BENARES

THE STRONGHOLD OF HINDUISM

BENARES

THE STRONGHOLD OF HINDUISM

C. PHILLIPS CAPE

GYAN

Published by

GYAN

Gyan Publishing House
5, Ansari Road
Daryaganj, New Delhi-110002
Phone: 011-47034999, 9811692060
E-mail: books@gyanbooks.com

Distribution Network
gyanbooks.com
India, USA, Canada, UK, Australia

ISBN: 978-93-6780-164-2 (HB)

First Published, 1910

2nd Impression 2024

Printed at: Gyan Press, Delhi.

BENARES THE STRONGHOLD OF HINDUISM
Author: C. PHILLIPS CAPE

Frontispiece] BENARES. [*Photo by Saeed Bros., Benares*

BENARES

THE STRONGHOLD OF HINDUISM

BY

REV. C. PHILLIPS CAPE

BENARES, INDIA

London

CHARLES H. KELLY

25-35 CITY ROAD, AND 26 PATERNOSTER ROW, E.C.

PREFACE

Some of these short sketches have been published in the *Foreign Field*, the *Indian Methodist Times*, and *At Home and Abroad.* Most of them, however, now appear in print for the first time. A few of the chapters have been written specially for young people.

I wish to express my indebtedness to the Rev. WALTER SEED, of Windsor, for seeing these pages through the press ; and I must not forget to thank Mr. Saced, of Benares, for his splendid photographs.

C. P. C.

CONTENTS

Contents

LIST OF ILLUSTRATIONS

Illustrations

A STREET IN BENARES CITY.

[Photo by Rev. A. T. Cape

BENARES.

CHAPTER I.

BENARES.

BENARES lies on the left or northern bank of the Ganges, about seventy-five miles below its junction with the Jamna at Allahabad. It is one of the oldest cities in the world, and one of the wealthiest cities of India.

Benares was famous before Rome was known, and for many centuries has claimed and gained the homage of every devout Hindu. It is the Oxford and Mecca of Hinduism. Its river, its temples, its banks, are known and revered throughout India. Its very air and soil are counted holy. Residence in the city ensures salvation, death there makes salvation doubly sure.

Such is the reputed sanctity of Benares,

that its pandits are prepared to admit that should a Moslem or a Christian die within the limits of the city, he might reasonably hope to be saved!

Benares has about fifteen hundred temples, and more idols than inhabitants, although they number well over two hundred thousand.

To visit the holy city, to pray at her shrines, and to bathe in her river, is the highest ambition of every good Hindu. So the streets are daily thronged with pilgrims from every country in the vast peninsula, who have in Benares a visible embodiment of the strength of Hinduism which is absolutely unique, and to them, wonderfully imposing. The late Mr. Caine described this city as 'without question the most picturesque in India.'

Benares is the Jerusalem of the Hindu. As the Jews delighted to reside in their holy city, so every wealthy merchant and prince who professes the Hindu religion wishes to buy or build a house for himself at Benares.

There are palaces scattered throughout the city, but most of them are by the river. The owners visit them from time to time, and will count themselves happy if they die in the holy place. The temples, palaces, pinnacles, shrines, towers, and minarets, combine to make what the late Sir Richard Temple described as 'the finest river frontage in India.'

From the temples and palaces, leading down to the water side, are the spacious steps of the forty-seven 'ghāts' or bathing places and quays, for which Benares is famous.

The city has a few fine streets, but most of its children are packed away in the evil-smelling lanes—21,000 souls to the square mile.

It is reputed that there are 20,000 Brahmans in Benares. There are generally six European ordained missionaries. Christian work under such conditions will necessarily be difficult. But it should be remembered that we have in this city absolutely unparalleled opportunities for making our Lord known. When Buddha desired to win the people of India to his Way, he established himself in Benares. When Mrs. Annie Besant desired to vitalize Hinduism, she made Benares her head quarters. And from Benares she has sent forth her catechisms and disciples, teaching the people a higher morality than Hinduism ever knew. Paul lived and preached in the great cities, and the Church cannot afford to-day to be inadequately represented where the enemy is most subtle and strong.

If only Benares could be won for Christ, more than Benares would be won.

RAMNAGAR—THE PALACE OF THE MAHARAJAH OF BENARES.

[*Photo by Rev. A. T. Cape*

CHAPTER II.

BRAVE MEN.

In 1781 Warren Hastings came to Benares. He had ordered Rājā Cheit Singh to furnish one thousand horsemen to assist in the war against the French in the south. 'This he refused or omitted to do, and was fined by Warren Hastings £500,000.' So on the 14th of August, the Governor-General himself appeared on the scene, and took up his residence in the garden of Mādho Dās in the city. The next day Hastings asked the Rājā for a full account of his conduct. As the reply was considered unsatisfactory and offensive, Cheit Singh was put under arrest in his own house at Shiwāla ghāt. Warren Hastings himself tells us what happened next:—

'Intelligence came that large bodies of armed men had crossed the river from Rāmnagar, and had proceeded to the

Rājā's house. What follows is a scene of such horror, that it is with the greatest reluctance I submit to the painful duty of relating it. The guard over the Rājā consisted of two companies of Grenadier Sepoys, as above mentioned, from Major Popham's detachment, commanded by the officers already named, who were stationed in an enclosed square which surrounded the apartment where the Rājā was. The Resident's guard had returned with him. Major Popham sent another company of Sepoys under an officer, with ammunition to reinforce and support the first party. When the latter arrived at the Rājā's house they found it surrounded, and all the avenues blockaded by a multitude of armed men who opposed their passage. The minds of this tumultuous assembly becoming soon inflamed, some of them began to fire upon the Sepoys within the square ; and immediately, as if this had been a concerted signal, made an instantaneous and fierce attack on the Sepoys, who, wanting their accustomed means of defence, being without ammunition, were capable of making but a feeble resistance, and fell an easy sacrifice to the superior numbers of their assailants, who cut almost every man of this unfortunate party to pieces. The officers, it is supposed were the first victims to their fury, but not until they had by astonishing efforts of bravery, and undismayed amidst the imminent danger which surrounded them, involved a much superior number of their enemies in their fate. In the midst of this confusion the Rājā found means to escape through a wicket which opened to the river, and the banks being exceedingly steep in that place, he let himself down by turbans tied together, into a boat which was waiting for him, and conveyed him to the opposite shore,' to Rāmnagar, where the present Māharājāh resides.

Major Popham, in his official account of this disorder, gives the number of killed and wounded as 206. He adds, 'The bodies of Lieuts. Stalker, Scott and Symes were lying within a small distance of each other, shockingly mangled, and without any signs of life.'

Near the Cheit Ganj police station is an enclosed ground where the Sepoys were buried. Outside is a slab with the following inscription: 'The enclosed ground was the burial-place of brave men who died in the performance of their duty on the 16th of August, 1781, A.D. This wall was built to protect the spot from desecration, A.D. 1862.'

Close to the Shivālā Fort are the graves of the three lieutenants. On one of the tombs we read: 'This tablet has been erected by the Government N.W.P. to preserve the last earthly resting-place of Lieut. Arch. Scott, 1st Battalion Sepoys, Jer. Symes, 2nd Battalion Sepoys, J. Stalker, Resd. Body Guard, who were killed August 17, 1781, near this spot, doing their duty.'

Not far from our Mission bungalow is a large house called Nandesur Kothi. It belongs to the Māharājāh of Benares, and was lent by him to the Prince and Princess of Wales when they visited Benares in 1906. On the outside of the house is a marble slab, on which are inscribed the following words: 'This house was the residence of Mr. Davies, magistrate of Benares. It was defended by him single-handed with a spear on the 14th January, 1799, against 200 armed men led by the rebel Nawāb Wazīr Alī.'

The incident is worth recording at length, as it is given by the Rev. A. Parker, L.M.S., in his hand-book of Benares.

'In 1799 British affairs in India were in a very critical condition. In the south, Tippoo Sultan was gathering his forces for that last struggle which ended in his overthrow and death at Seringapatam in May. The French, maddened by their crushing defeat by Nelson at the battle of the Nile, were doing all in their power to harry and weaken their rivals in India. In the north a large Afghan army under Zamān Khān at Lahore was threatening a descent on the plains.

'It was at this critical moment that the insurrection of Wazīr Alī, the deposed Nawāb of Oudh occurred at Benares. Wazīr Alī had in 1791 been appointed to succeed his reputed father as Nawāb of

Oudh, but had within a year been deposed on the ground of illegitimacy, profligacy, and general disaffection, and sent to Benares, on the border of his kingdom, where he lived in sulky retirement on a large pension. Ever since his deposition he had nursed the idea of revenge. He was only nineteen years of age, and of the most arrogant temper and vicious habits. He never moved abroad without a large armed retinue, and disdained intercourse with all Europeans except Mr. Cherry, the British Resident at that time. From his residence in Mādho Dās's garden he kept up a correspondence with the Afghan army at Lahore, and had a whole circle of confederates at work concerting rebellion in the city and district. In several of the large houses in the city arms were collected, and at Pindrah Kot, a fortress fifteen miles outside Benares, a force was gathered to attack, at the favourable moment, the British troops encamped near by. The city was at that time in the most turbulent state. It was infested by a species of swaggering bully called Bānkās, so named from the peculiar curved dagger they carried, in the use of which they were very expert. These rogues lived on blackmail which they extorted from the more peaceable citizens, and were ready to join Wazīr Alī or any one else who could hold out to them promise of plunder. Early in January, when all their plans were laid and the conspirators were only waiting for the signal from the commander of the Lahore Army, there came an order from the Governor-General, through Mr. Cherry, that Wazīr Alī should be immediately removed to Calcutta. Naturally the Wazīr was deeply chagrined and discomfited, and determined on attempting a rising at once, hoping for revenge if not for success. On the 14th of January, 1799, he set out with his usual large retinue to visit Mr. Cherry, who then occupied the building now used as the Collector's kachahri. On the way he met Mr. Davies, the magistrate and his wife, mounted on an elephant returning from their morning ride. Wazīr Alī's business was not with them just at that moment, and so after the usual salutations, they were allowed to pass, but not before Mr. Davies' sharp eye had detected something unusual in the number and array of the retinue. On his arrival at Mr. Cherry's house Wazīr Alī was received in a friendly manner and offered a cup of tea, which he declined. Then, as Mr. Cherry continued his morning meal, he began in an angry tone to complain of the recent order ; and at last, suddenly jumping up, he seized Mr. Cherry and dealt him a blow with his dagger. This was regarded as the signal for action by his followers, and the unfortunate man was immediately attacked from all sides. He managed, however, to break away from his assailants, but was followed and killed a few yards from the house. With him fell Mr. Evans, his secretary, and Captain Conway, who rode unsuspectingly up to the house while the disturbance was proceeding. The Wazīr then collected his followers and moved off to Nandesar Kothī, the residence of Mr. Davies. On the way they met and killed in his palanquin, Mr.

Hill, who kept a shop in the city. In the meantime Mr. Davies, alarmed at the threatening aspect of Wazir Ali's retinue, had immediately on his arrival home despatched a note of warning to Mr. Cherry, which however, arrived too late. Being on the alert he saw the first of Wazīr Alī's followers approach his house and fire on his servants. There was not a moment to be lost, and, unable to get any other weapon, he snatched a spear from an attendant at the door and directed Mrs. Davies to ascend to the roof, taking with her the one child who remained below. The staircase they ascended was narrow and winding, and covered in at the top with a trap-door of bamboo and matting. Over this Mr. Davies mounted guard to defend it, if possible, against this band of desperate men. The spear he had was no mean weapon. The shaft was of iron, plated with silver in rings to give a firm grasp, rather more than six feet in length and furnished with a long triangular blade of more than twenty inches, with sharp edges. The first man who attempted to make his way up the staircase was greeted with a sharp lunge of the spear, and hastily retreated with a badly-wounded arm. The second, more wary, avoided the spear, and grasping the blade with both his hands tried to wrest it out of Mr. Davies' grasp ; but he, dropping the shaft on the edge of the door and using it as a lever, tore it out of his assailant's hands, which were severely cut by the sharp edges of the blade. After this no further attempt was made to force the stair, though many bullets were fired up the staircase and horsemen rode round the house on every side trying to get a shot at the occupants of the roof. Thus for nearly two hours, like another Leonidas at his Thermopylae, did this brave man keep at bay a murderous band of two hundred desperadoes.

'In the meantime the other Europeans had sought shelter, and one of them, Mr. Cleves, had, on a swift horse and by a circuitous route ridden to where, ten miles away, General Erskine's force was encamped. There he met with a troop of cavalry just returned from exercise, and to their officer he communicated his news. The word of command was at once given, and the force wheeled round and set off for Benares at a gallop. When the thunder of their hoofs was heard, Wazīr Alī sullenly drew off his men and retired to his retreat in Mādho Dās's garden. Before night fell the garden had been attacked and Wazīr Alī forced to flee by unfrequented ways northwards to Azimgarh. For nearly a year he maintained himself in the wild country at the foot of the Himalayas, but he was eventually captured, and the first anniversary of his unsuccessful rebellion saw him carried as a prisoner through Benares to Calcutta.'

The lower portion of the staircase defended by Mr. Davies may still be seen in the Nandesur Kothi, and in the old cemetery at Chauka Ghāt is a colossal monument to Mr. Cherry and his friends. It is in the form of a square pointed obelisk, set on an immense platform of stone, ornamented at the four corners by large funeral urns. It has the following inscription, which is of recent date:—

'This obelisk was erected in memory of George Frederick Cherry, Esq., G.G.'s Agent; Captain Conway; Robert Graham, Esq.; Richard Evans, Esq.; who were murdered by Wazīr Alī, January 14, 1799.'

In 1857 came the great mutiny. At Benares two thousand native troops and about two hundred British soldiers were stationed.

Dr. Fitchett tells the story in graphic words:

'Nowhere, perhaps, did English courage shine out with a clearer flame than at Benares. Benares is the holy city of Hinduism; it had a population of 300,000, fanatical and turbulent in the highest degree. The Cantonment was held by three Sepoy regiments—all pledged to revolt—150 men of a British regiment, the 10th, and some thirty British gunners, with half a battery of artillery, under the command of Olpherts. But the cluster of soldiers and civilians responsible for the city—Tucker the commissioner,

Frederick Gubbins the judge, Lind the magistrate, Ponsonby the brigadier, and Olpherts in command of the guns—held on to their post; by mere cool audacity kept the turbulent city in awe, and the mutinous sepoys from breaking out; and sent on to other parts in greater peril than their own such scanty reinforcements of British troops as reached them. In the Commissioner, Tucker, at least, this heroic courage had a religious root. "The twenty-second chapter of 2 Samuel," he wrote to Lord Canning, "was their stand-by." . .

'Neil reached the city on June 3, and found himself on the very edge of a tragedy. The sepoys had arranged for an outbreak on the night of June 4. The native troops numbered over 2,000; the British troops, as we have seen, consisted of 150 men of the 10th, and thirty artillerymen with three guns. To these Neil added sixty of his "Lambs" whom he had brought with him. Neil put the impress of his vehement will on the brigadier, Ponsonby, in charge of the station, and at half an hour's notice it was resolved to disarm the Sepoys.

'The business was ill-managed. The sepoys commenced to shoot, the Sikhs turned on their officers. Ponsonby, an old man, found "the sun" and the strain of the scene too much for him, and visibly broke down. He dismounted, and Neil, who had been grimly watching the scene, said abruptly, "General, I assume command." Ponsonby assented in silence, and Neil instantly opened on the mutineers with grape and musketry fire, and, after a few minutes' furious shooting, Sikh and sepoy fled. The 250, that is, destroyed, in a military sense, the 2,000!' (*Tale of the Mutiny*).

To-day there are only 140 British soldiers in Benares, and no more are needed, for the people are content, they are unarmed, and we have the railways.

THE WORSHIP OF GANESHA.
Photo by Rev. A. T. Cape]

A VISION OF UGLINESS:
THE GREAT GOD GANESHA.

[*Photo by Rev. A. T. Cape*

CHAPTER III.

ONE OF THE GODS.

HIS name is Ganesha or Ganpati. He is also called Puliyār, 'the son,' in some parts of India. His father was Shiva and his mother Pārvatī. You will wonder why he has an elephant's head, and this is the explanation as given by some of the learned men. They say that one day an evil spirit looked at him, the result being that his head was burnt off. His mother began to cry, and to console her, one of the great gods said that her son could have the head of the first thing she met when she went out; and it so happened that she met with the very evil spirit who had caused her grief. He had an elephant's head, which was immediately transferred to her son's shoulders.

He has only one tusk, as the other was broken off while fighting with a demon.

But he has four arms and hands, and in these he holds a necklace, a mace, a lotus, and a big piece of sweetmeat called 'laḍḍu.' He is supposed to be very fond of sweets and able to swallow at least twenty-one pieces of 'laḍḍu' at one sitting. That is the reason why he is so fat. He is a greedy god; but he is very popular because he is supposed to give good luck to all who worship him. When the Hindu begins a journey, or commences to build a house, or to write a book, he asks Ganesha to help him by keeping away all the evil spirits who might wish to do harm either to him and his work.

Many of the gods and goddesses of India have animals upon which to ride. Ganesha is supposed to ride on a rat, which is therefore regarded by many as a sacred animal—too holy to be killed, even when it spreads the plague. The rat is often carved beneath the god, as you can see from the photograph. Ganesha, when worshipped, is adorned with garlands of marigolds and jasmine, and other flowers are offered to him. The boy who is pouring the water on his head is one of his devotees. He has got the water from the well of knowledge which is just behind him. The water of this well is said to be very pleasing to the gods, because the great god Shiva took refuge in it, when the Moslem emperor Aurangzeb demolished his temple. The priests who are watching the boy are wearing their sacred threads. When they worship the saints they wear the thread like a necklace; when they are praying for their ancestors the sacred cord is put over the right shoulder and under the left; and when the gods are worshipped the thread is worn over the left and under the right shoulder. This thread can only be used by the Brahmans, the Kshatriyās, and the Vaishyas, that is, by the high castes. But not even high-caste women are allowed to wear it. Those who are entitled to use this sacred thread are called the 'twice-born.' This cord can be bought by anybody in the bazaar. It consists of three fine white cotton threads twisted together and tied by a special knot. But the 'twice-born' cannot wear this thread until it has been consecrated by the priests.

One of the Brahmans sitting close by the image of Ganesha is wearing a necklace of beads. These sometimes consist of the berries of a tree, and are 108 in number. Some of the people say that they are not really berries, but the tears of the god Shiva, which he shed one day when he was in a great temper!

There is one very ugly image of Ganesha in Benares. It is called 'The Seeker.' The story is that Shiva was expelled from the 'holy city' by the order of a prince. Ganesha heard of the god's exile and came to Benares to help him. The prince was so devout, that although Ganesha sought to find occasion against him as touching his religion, he could find no error or fault in him; but having come to Benares, he finally decided that he could not do better than reside there permanently.

It is very sad to see multitudes of men and women bowing down before this red, deformed god. But as they want help and have not heard of Jesus Christ they make their appeal to this vision of ugliness. To the left of the god is a small conch, a marine shell, probably from the West Indian islands. It is supposed by the Hindus to be the body of a sea-demon who fought with Vishnu, who slew him, and used his bones as a trumpet to terrify his enemies! The conch is blown in the temples to please the deities and to arouse them when asleep. The small shells are filled with the holy water, which is poured over the images of the gods.

CHAPTER IV.

THE MONKEY TEMPLE.

It is generally understood by Europeans that the Hindu will on no account take life; and indeed, by many of them, such an act is counted the great sin. But in the temple raised to Durga, multitudes of goats are sacrificed. The animal's head is fastened to the ground, its hind legs are lifted high in the air, and then, with one blow, the creature is decapitated. The head is placed by the officiating priest on a small altar close to the shrine. The animal's body is then removed, to be eaten by the vegetarian Hindu!

These hideous sacrifices are offered to the goddess, with the hope that by them she will be propitiated, and will look with favour upon the petitioner's request. An educated Indian offers the explanation that the goat is sacrificed because it repre-

THE MONKEY TEMPLE.

sents the lower passions of man, and as the sinful self must be slain before the deity can be approached, this is done symbolically by the offering up of the goat.

Durga's former name, the Hindus say, was Gaurī, which she changed to Durga, to commemorate her victory over the famous demon Durg.

The splendid tank and temple built by Rānī Bhawānī have made Durga's shrine one of the most popular in temple-possessed Benares. Every Tuesday the people throng to it in large numbers, and twice a year, in March and August, there are religious festivals, attended by many thousands of excited devotees.

The temple is beautifully carved, and its steeple is surrounded by a number of small cupolas, each of which ends in a gilded point. In the porch hangs a massive bell, which the priests affirm was the gift of a European magistrate. Outside the courtyard is the 'Naubat-Khāna,' in which a large kettle-drum is beaten in honour of the goddess. To the left is the

specially delight to honour. 'Bande Mātāram,' 'Hail! my mother,' is their invocation to the goddess. 'Hail! motherland,' is a free translation preferred by some patriots. One can easily understand that they should love their motherland rather than the skull-girdled goddess of blood.

CHAPTER V.

THE WORSHIP OF VISHNU AND SHIVA

THE image of Vishnu, who is the second in the Hindu triad, is made of stone, brass, silver or gold, and is put up on a small brass platform. It is then bathed by the worshipper. When this is done, he puts some sandal-wood on the god's forehead. Then a leaf of the sacred tulsi plant is presented to the image. 'The tulsi is very commonly worshipped by the followers of Vishnu, and the plant is most carefully tended as his representative. Every morning the ground near it is cleaned with cow-dung and water; at night a lamp is hung before it. During the two hottest months of the year, a vessel of water is placed over it, so that it constantly receives moisture. When a plant dies, it is cast into a river, the same honour being given to it as to an image, as soon as the worship of it is concluded. It is a common custom to place a sprig of tulsi near the head of a dying person.'

THE SACRIFICIAL GOAT.

[*Photo dy Saeed Bros., Benares.*

Beside the tulsi, many sweet-scented flowers are presented to the god. Then incense is burnt before the idol. After this a lamp is lit and waved in a circle in front of the image. As the god is supposed by this time to be hungry, he is fed with sweets behind a screen. The conch is sounded, and Vishnu is said to be specially pleased with its noise. While the bathing is going on and the light being waved, a bell is tinkled. During the burning of the incense, beads are counted and hymns repeated. When the worship is finished, the image is put away in a safe place, and the offerings are eaten by the worshippers.

'In the temple of Māhadeo (Shiva), there are generally two or more officiating priests who appropriate to their own use the offerings made to the god. After bathing, people visit the temple, take with them water in their brazen jugs, and pour it over the image, which is generally on a wooden stand; the water that is poured on it is received in a trough, and runs out of the temple through a small drain. After

the purpose the photograph of an absent friend does. You may ask him how the ludicrous and dreadful images of Ganesha and Kali can kindle helpful thoughts of the Deity; and you may tell him that while you yourself do not feel the need of images, as the Roman Catholic does, their images are of good men and women, whose memory is a stimulus to noble thought and action.

When the stone image has been carved, the Brahman priest is called and a special life-giving ceremony is performed, which results, we are told, in the god coming to reside in a special way in the stone. Then the image is cared for as if it were actually alive. It is bathed, it is fed, it is fanned, it is put to bed, it is protected from the mosquitoes with curtains, and altogether it is treated as if it were really a living god—a living Hindu god. If the image is of Krishna, an incarnation of Vishnu, it may one day be married to the sacred tulsi plant! So you see it looks as though some Hindus think their gods are something more than photographs!

CHAPTER VI.

THE DEMON'S HEAD.

'PISHĀCH-MOCHAN' is the name of a famous tank in Benares. Pishāch means demon, and Mochan deliverance.

The people say that once upon a time a brave bad demon tried to get into the sacred city of Benares. As soon as the gods who lived on the spot heard of his approach they did all they could to stop him. But as he was a very strong demon he was able to beat them all and then entered the city. He went on until he reached the place which is now called Pishāch-Mochan, where there is a very big pond. Here he was met by a city watchman called Bhaironāth. The watchman and the demon fought together, and at last the demon was defeated, and, like Goliath, had his head cut off by his conqueror.

The watchman carried off the head to

THE GOBLIN'S HEAD. [*Photo by Saeed Bros., Benares*

show to his master, whose name was Bisheshwar. When he had finished his story, the demon's head began to speak, and besought Bisheshwar not to send him away out of the city but to let him stay where his head had been cut off. Bisheshwar consented, on the understanding that the demon should not allow any other evil spirit to enter the city. It was also agreed that all those pilgrims who intended to visit the holy city of Gaya should first pay a visit to the demon.

Many thousands of people visit the tank every year to pay their respect to the great goblin, whose big ugly stone head is placed by the road-side and close to the water. Why do they worship the goblin? Because they think that he can deliver them from all the other evil spirits who may try to do them harm. 'Why don't they go to the great God, Parameshwar, and beg him to save them from all the spirits, goblins, demons, ghosts, and ghouls they so much fear?' an Indian priest was asked. 'They don't want to trouble God by referring such small matters to him,' was the reply. And then we thought of some words of Ruskin, 'There is nothing so small but that we may honour God by asking His guidance of it.'

But in truth, to be delivered from the fear of evil spirits would be no small matter to the Hindu, who thinks that the loss of money, health, friends, and life are all caused by these malignant foes. To tell them of a Father in heaven who loves and protects His children, is to bring very good news to these ignorant, harassed souls.

TEMPLES, PALACES, AND PILGRIMS AT BENARES.

CHAPTER VII.

JUGGERNAUT.

In Benares there is a small shrine sacred to Jagannāth, 'containing three figures of horrible ugliness. On the right is Jagannāth, on the left is his brother Balbhadrā, and, in the middle, is their sister Subhadrā. The former have arms but no hands or feet; while the latter is destitute of arms as well as of feet. These large-mouthed, goggle-eyed, round-faced deities are equal in frightfulness to some of the idols made and worshipped by the savages of the Fiji Islands in the South Seas.' This is the description of a missionary. You can now read an account of a visit to the world-famous shrine of Jagannāth, given by a Hindu in an Indian magazine.

'A friend of mine being desirous of visiting Shri Jagannāthjī, persuaded me to accompany him to Puri. On reaching Puri, the instant we moved out of the sheltering train, we were beset by a crowd of questioning pandyas (temple priests), who one and all seemed desirous of knowing everything about our parentage, birth-place, the names of our ancestors, and our caste, &c. These proceedings might appear queer to an outsider, but every Indian knows that he will be met by a crowd of pandyas whenever he goes to a holy place in India, and that he will be claimed by some one of them as his special shish (customer), on the strength of a signature of one of his ancestors. We proclaimed aloud our names, and also told the crowd that we were the ancestral property of such and such a pandya, and that he alone could take us in charge. After a couple of minutes one man came up and informed us that he was the agent of the pandya we sought, and that he was detailed on duty at the station, to receive the sheep belonging to their spiritual shepherd, his master, and so saying took us in charge.

'We then drove into the city, and secured lodgings close by the great temple door, called the Sinha Darwāja (the Lion Gate).

'Here we put away our travelling gear, and after taking off everything that had a suspicion of leather about it, started for the night darshan (spectacle).

'We joined the crowd at the door, and moving on slowly, went into the inner temple. Here two large misshapen statues of wood were pointed out as representatives of Krishna and Balarāma, and a smaller one as that of Subhadrā, their sister.

'All around were fat and well-fed pandyas who exhorted the pilgrims to offer up as much as possible of their goods, and to exchange their perishable worldly gear for large and lasting treasures in the worlds to come.

'We stood and listened, till, unable to resist such arguments any longer, we, too, parted with the silver we had about us, and returned home, followed by the blessings of the pandyas.

'When we came back, we found that

some prasād (offering) had been sent for us by the pandya, and that it was composed of rice and dāl, &c., and I was told that it was customary for all to eat out of the same dish, without any restriction, in Jagannāth. Knowing how strict is the Indian system regarding the eating of food cooked by the hands of those not belonging to the same caste, I was astonished to see the Brāhman pandya eat out of the same dish set before a Bengali, a Panjabi or a U.P. man, and it seems that not even the most orthodox Brahman of up-country ever dreams of refusing to partake of such food. It is said that nobody in Puri cooks for himself, except of course the foreign officers. Every Hindu purchases his food from the temple. Our pandya was much disturbed when he found that I was not going to eat that food, but when he found me obdurate he did not try to persuade me any further.

'Next day we went wandering round and round the temple, and found clear signs that though the modern worship in the temple is Vaishnava in its character, yet the old system must have been purely Shākta, as the statues and paintings on the temple wall testified. It is said also that a former Rājā of Orissa was converted by the great Saint and Bhakta, Shri Chaitanya Mahāprabhu, from Shākti worship to Vaishnavism, which is a purer form of worship. Though the pandyas claim that the worship of Krishna and Balarāma has been continued ever since the building of the temple, certain old ceremonies and forms of worship that still continue, notably the interdining of all castes, clearly point out that the old worship was to Shākti Devī.

'Continuing my wanderings, I came across a Nanakshahi temple, where Granth Saheb was worshipped. Close by is a place where pieces of cake are distributed to all the pilgrims in the name of Dāsa Malkūa, who was also a great devotee. After finishing our morning outing we came home, and found that we had been stolen ; I don't mean that some one had put us in his pocket and walked off, but that our real pandya was somebody else, and that the agent of another pandya had secured us, or rather our offerings, for his master under the name of the real one. But the agent of our real pandya was on the look-out, and he quietly brought up to us the old books which contained the signatures of our ancestors, and established his rights clearly; we were therefore compelled to give up our first priest, who was also made to disgorge his priestly plunder under the threat of being reported to the police. We parted with the first priest with a heavy heart, as he had called down many a spiritual curse on us for having retaken a gift from a Brahman, but presently picked up courage again, when our priest told us that such curses mattered not, as they were levelled at us by one who had no spiritual jurisdiction over us, and that he alone had the real right of either blessing or banning us.'

Jagannāth is supposed to be an appearance of Vishnu, the second god of the Hindu triad. 'There is however, considerable reason for doubting whether originally Jagannāth—the Lord of the

World—had any connexion with Vishnu. It is possible that he was the local divinity of some now unknown tribe, whose worship was engrafted into Hinduism, and the new god, when admitted into the Pantheon, was regarded as another manifestation of Vishnu; or what is more probable, as Puri was a head-centre of Buddhism, when that system was placed under a ban and its followers persecuted, the temple was utilized for Hinduism, and Jagannath, nominally a Hindu deity, was really Buddhistic.'

It has been suggested too, that the fact that all castes can eat together at Jagannāth, though nowhere else, may confirm our suspicion that the worship of this god is of Buddhist origin. At the time of the car festival, the image of the god is drawn through the streets by excited crowds, who hope to gain salvation by rendering such assistance.

CHAPTER VIII.

THE INDIAN SANDOW.

THE Hindus say that Bhīma was the son of Prithā and Vāyu. He and his four brothers are well known to the people of India. The five brothers were called the Pāndavas. How bravely and fiercely they fought against the Kurus, their cousins, is written in one of the sacred books of India, called the Mahābhārata.

When Bhīma was a small boy, one of his cousins tried to poison him, and then threw him into the water. 'Bhīma, however, was not drowned, but descended to the abode of the serpent demons, who freed him from the poison, and gave him a liquid to drink, which made him as strong as ten thousand snake-devils. From that moment he became a second Hercules.'

Bhīma is said to have been very large, very cruel, very bad-tempered, and very greedy. When the dinner was ready, he had half, and what was left, his four brothers had to share!

It is said he was very fond of his mother and brothers; but we are also told that his selfishness, pride, and too great love of pleasure, caused his death.

There is a lake in the hills of North India sacred to Bhīma. The people say that the peculiar fish found there are lice from his body!

Some of the savage tribes of India worship him in the form of a big piece of stone daubed with paint. The royal family of Nepal count him worthy of special honour. His name means 'the terrible one.' He has another name, Bhimsen, and that means, 'He who has a terrible army.'

I want all of you who read about this Hindu Sandow to pray that the boys and girls of India who worship him may learn that *he* is the strong man who can conquer himself.

CHAPTER IX.

BY THE RIVER-SIDE.

'We haven't seen any little girls thrown into the river,' said a lady to me, in a seemingly disappointed tone, as we disembarked at Rāj ghāt.

It was quite true. Not even a crocodile had appeared! But though the British Rāj and public opinion have put an end to what might be an attraction to a certain type of tourist, there still remain things worthy of the kodak and the notebook.

One morning we saw two vultures resting in mid-stream, upon what appeared to be a corpse. As the boat drew near, a curious spectacle was witnessed. The two vultures fell into the water, and being unable to fly away, had to swim ashore. It was as much as they could manage, for as they slowly beat away the water

THE FASCINATION OF THE RIVER.

[*Photo by Saeed Bros., Benares*

with their long wings, it was very clear they were not in their proper element. One vulture landed on the north side, and was met by a crowd of small boys, who did not pelt it with stones. The other bird's approach was witnessed by a number of vultures, who seemed deeply interested in its struggles, and must have been painfully disappointed by its vitality on landing. We reached the corpse—to find it was a cow!

Swimming vultures are not a part of the regular river programme; but the bathers and the burning ghat, the well of salvation, and the minarets of Aurangzeb's mosque can always be relied on. The Kedārnāth ghāt is patronized by the Bengalis. That these people have great faith in the antiseptic properties of the sacred stream is clear from the fact that they go on drinking its water, although close by a huge city sewer belches forth its filth.

On a small bamboo platform, in front of the steps, are the holy men; some muttering over their beads, some reading their Sanskrit books; others sitting as still as death, longing for their emancipation.

On the banks of the river is the Nepaulese temple, which is worth a visit if only to see a sample of the style of carving which an indulgent government permits, in deference to the religious susceptibilities of the people.

Most of our friends from a distance are disappointed with the burning ghāt. It is all so sordid and mean. Pierre Loti, speaking of one corpse he saw, tells us: '*Elle etait adorablement jolie.*' Let no one, deceived by this, go to Jalsain ghāt for loveliness. The sight is repellent to the last degree. A stack of wood, with a thin dry corpse in the midst. When the wood is wet, or the wind is high, the work is painfully slow. Then the burners of the dead lift their long poles and break the smouldering bones. Happily, or unhappily, no one seems to care. Hungry and inquisitive dogs add a dreadful horror to the scene. If the fire fails—then comes their turn

The mourners, who are as silent as the thing they watch, sit huddled about on the steps above; quiet now that the angry bargaining with the wood-sellers is over, and they have done their best for the dead. 'Ram is true, Ram is true!' comes down the narrow lane above, to be followed in a moment by something in white or red, which, in its turn, must pass through the fire and water.

The burning ghāt has been busy lately. In one week 82,000 people in India have died in all the agonies of plague. The corpses are carried swiftly through the city down to the river. The face is uncovered, and into the gaping lips the soul-purifying water is poured. Then the pyre and the fire and once more the water. Life is common and death is very common in India. When one has many lives to live and many deaths to die, one life and one death do not count for much, the Hindu may argue.

As we pass on, we notice the footprints of Vishnu, carved in white marble; 'Here rājās are burnt,' says the officiating priest, 'and here Europeans always give bakhshish.'

'It is a recent invention of the covetous Brahman,' replied one of our party in Hindī, and to this the crowd laughingly assents, as they make way for us to move towards the Manikarnikā well, which contains the holiest water of the holiest city in India. It was filled originally, some say, with the sweat of Vishnu; but the tank has been cleaned out since then, and at present contains nothing but water and mud and milk and flowers and rice and—'attar' of humanity.

Behind the railings at the back of the tank, the unedifying spectacle can often be seen of a greedy priest trying to squeeze a few more pice from some poor peasant, who has already paid heavily for the privilege of immersion in the sacred filth. 'This is the place,' says Dr. Sherring, 'sought after by the thousands of pilgrims flocking yearly to the holy city, who are drawn to it by a mysterious and irresistable fascination. Its fetid water is regarded as a healing balm, which will infallibly wash away all the sins of the soul, and make it pure and holy. There is no sin so heinous or abominable, but, in popular estimation, it is here instantly effaced. Even for the crime of murder, it can, it is said, procure forgiveness. No wonder, therefore, that conscience-stricken sinners should rush to this well from all quarters, and, deluding themselves by its reputed sanctity, should by the easy process of washing in its foulness, seek to atone, in one minute, for the crimes and sins of a life-time. Yet it is appalling to think that the human soul, thus conscious of its guilt, and perhaps in many instances, in agony respecting it, and anxious for pardon, and for reconciliation with God, should be so cruelly mocked and deceived.'

We return to our boat by the Scindia ghāt, which, had it been finished, would have been one of the most beautiful of the river-side buildings. But the foundations were inadequate and the ruin great.

As we look along the banks, we see that the healing river is the great destroyer.

Listen to Pierre Loti: '*Quel infatigable destructeur, le Gange! Tant de palais écroulés dans ses eaux! Des façades entières ont glissé, sont descendues sans se rompre et demeurent là, à demi noyées. Et tant de temples! Ceux d'en bas, qui voisinent trop avec le fleuve, ont toutes leurs pyramides penchées comme des tours de Pise, sapées en dessous irrémédiablement.*'

The most striking edifice on the banks of the Ganges is Aurangzeb's mosque, a painful reminder to the Hindu of the ways of their former rulers. Ascend the minarets. This wonderful city, with its two hundred thousand souls, is now at our feet. In the distance can be seen Sārnāth, the birthplace of Buddhism. Outside the gate of the mosque sits a sādhu on a bed of spikes. When he dies, he will not be burnt like common men. He needs no purification by fire. He will be wrapped in a piece of sackcloth, a stone will be tied to his legs, and he will be dropped into the river. But in spite of the dead saint, the people will go on with their bathing, and drinking!

There they are—men, women, and children, from every country in India.

At last they have reached the holy city and the holy river. 'Ganga Jī' is worshipped with deepest reverence by every devout Hindu, who believes that she was born from the feet of the famous god Vishnu.

There are other sacred streams, but none possess such saving sanctity as mother Ganges is universally acknowledged to impart.

As the river breaks upon his view, the pilgrim uplifts his hands, and cries aloud in exultation, 'Victory to the adored Ganga!'

When the riverside is reached, he stoops down and sprinkles the holy water on his eyes and head. Then a priestly Brahman comes to direct him and says: 'Join your hands and I will recite a prayer.' And this is his address to the river: 'O Ganga, I salute your two feet, your two feet which are beautiful and which are worshipped by good and evil deities: O Ganga, according to their faith, thou givest present happiness and final release to all.'

The pilgrim is then ordered to take up some of the water in his hand and to listen to another prayer, which is a confession of sin. 'Now bathe,' says the priest, and the Hindu plunges under the healing stream. He readily gives the Brahman his fee, for he believes that mother Ganges has given him salvation: not the redemption we have in Christ, but a release from the ills of this life, a reduction in the number of the transmigrations, and a quick return to the Eternal Source.

The Brahmans sit quietly on their bamboo platforms. They restrain their breath while meditating. They pour out water to the goddess of the river in the name of the sun god.

They stand and worship the sun. Then they recite one of the oldest prayers in the world, the Gāyatri or Sāvitrī, 'Let us meditate on the excellent glory of the Divine Life-giving luminary; may he enlighten our minds.'

The Brahman considers these words

'THE HINDU WORSHIPS THE RIVER AND THE SUN.'

so sacred that he refuses to recite them in the presence of a low-caste man. When I asked my pandit to teach me to recite the prayer, he told me that he could not do so while he wore clothes which were ceremonially unclean. So I myself said the Sanskrit words as well as I could, and if I made a mistake, my pandit shook his head, and when I spoke correctly, he nodded his endorsement. And so I learnt the prayer. One day in a temple, sacred to Kāli, I ventured to repeat the words. Several of the Brahmans smiled, but one said, 'You rule the country; if you did not, I should cut your throat.' The temple policeman ordered the priest to be quiet, and the other priests laughed him into silence; but I perceived that my little knowledge of Sanskrit might be a dangerous thing if indiscreetly used.

By the river-side, the Hindu can be seen worshipping the river and the sun. Nature-worship, natural and noble, you may call it; but the Hindus, alas! worship the Brahman as well, and will drink the water in which he has bathed his feet.

They bathe in the Ganges because they have not heard of the cleansing love of Christ. For long centuries men and women have come to the river. And they have died—those countless multitudes—not knowing Christ.

I will tell you a story. Not many weeks ago, in a certain village, so many people died of plague that there were none left to burn the dead. There were some living, but they were panic-stricken, and so feared the plague, that they were unwilling to take those awful burdens to the river. And so the plague triumphed. But one of the men of that village went at night to the river-side, to burn the dreadful dead, to save the living; his perfect love cast out fear. He saved others, himself he could not save. The apostle John says, 'Every one that loveth, is begotten of God, and knoweth God,' and Jesus will say, 'Ye did it unto Me,' to those who have served His brethren.

THE HOLY MEN.

[*Photo by Saeed Bros., Benares*

CHAPTER X.

THE HOLY MEN.

UNFORTUNATELY for India, many of these men are notoriously unholy. This, at least, is the testimony of some respectable Indians. Instead of exhibiting an unselfish, self-controlled godly life to the common people, the ascetic's example is too often extremely pernicious. They always beg, they sometimes steal, they are rarely sober. They look like lunatics, they smell like sewers, they live like swine.

The last census revealed the fact that India can boast of having more than five millions of these 'saints.' Some of them become ascetics to attain power over nature and the gods; others from a fear of inability to conquer in life's battle; some, because they think they can obtain salvation by subduing the flesh; others because they wish to propitiate the unseen powers; some because they have a yearning for present communion with the divine, and others because they are 'criminals evading the clutches of justice.' In fact a Maharajah in North India says that 'amongst ascetics in this country nowadays, only a few true and respectable men, who have really relinquished all worldly desires and subdued their passions are to be found, as the majority of them are simply beggars, thieves, and bad characters . . . I have personally known cases where the police arrested amongst these Sannyāsis, men who were under warrant for a murder case, or belonged to a gang of decoits.'

Some of these men, probably the more sincere, think that they can benefit themselves by torturing their bodies. Here is one man sitting exposed to the heat of five fires; here is another reclining on a bed of spikes; and there are others who have taken a vow of silence—they gave the census enumerator a lot of trouble!—or load themselves with heavy chains, or hang suspended from a tree head downwards, or fast for days and mutilate themselves. One man in Benares had kept his right arm raised above his head, by the help of a bamboo stick, for so long a time, that the limb had become atrophied and useless, and the nails of his fingers pierced the palm of the hand.

Some think that they can purify their hearts by swallowing many yards of cloth and then withdrawing it. There is another of these holy men in Benares, who claims to be a devourer of filth and corpses. Some five hundred ascetics were allowed to parade in a public procession in a state of absolute nudity, last year at Allahabad.

Such are some of India's 'saints.' It is good to know that there are others, men whose lives are a witness to the fact that they believe in the existence and importance of the Unseen, and in the value of purity and self-control.

The ascetic system of India has 'tended toward the recognition of the equality of all Hindus, and has therefore been inimical to the rigid caste system so dear to the Brahman priesthood.' Any man, or woman, of any caste can become an ascetic.

In the year 1898 a government official reported that in the North-Western Provinces (now the United Provinces), one-twentieth of the population were religious beggars. Such a large proportion of non-producers must, of course, have an injurious effect upon the industrial condition of the people. An Indian magazine, dealing with this problem as it affects India, says that 'at the lowest calculation of three rupees (four shillings) per mensem for the support of each of the 5,200,000 professional beggars, about eighteen crores of rupees (£12,000,000) are annually spent by the workers of India for the maintenance of non-workers, the great majority of whom are utterly undeserving. If this vast charity were properly organized and spent on the education of the people, in religious and in secular, technical and industrial arts and sciences, what incalculable good could be done!'

There is also the political aspect of the question. Not a few of these sādhus wander about the country filling the ears of the villagers with damaging and false reports of the white people and the British government. They can easily be employed as spreaders of sedition, for they are here to-day and gone to-morrow, and the ignorant rustic will believe their tale.

It has sometimes been suggested that Christian missionaries, should, as far as possible, adopt the habits of these ascetics. There are two important objections to this suggestion. One is that the holy men of India, as a class, have not won the respect of the Indian people, and it would therefore be no gain to the missionary to be regarded as in any respect similar to the sādhus. Then again, the Christian minister's message is essentially different from the sādhus, for he does not call the people to copy the narrow, selfish, isolated life of the anchorite, but to emulate the philanthropic spirit of the Son of Man, who came, not to be served, but to serve, and to give His life for others.

CHAPTER XI.

SĀDHUS AT HOME.

THE gentleman on the spikes is 'At Home' to all comers. Whenever we meet, he is given a tract, a hymn-sheet, or a gospel in Hindi, which he receives with pleasure, and reads, we trust, to his profit. He spends a part of each morning studying the Rāmāyana, whilst occupying his uneasy seat. This nail-covered couch is said to be in memory of Bhishma, one of the heroes of the Mahābhārata, whose body was so pierced with arrows, that when he fell from his chariot they kept him from the ground.

Sādhus generally wear necklaces and carry rosaries, the magnetic influences of which are most helpful—so Mrs. Besant tells us.

The rosaries consist generally of 84 or 108 beads. In the *Journal of the Society*

"THE SĀDHU'S CALF FEARS NO PRODIGAL'S RETURN."

[*Photo by Saeed Bros., Benares*

of Arts for 1902, quoted by Mr. Oman in his fascinating book on the ascetics of India, there is an interesting reference to these rosaries. Sir George Birdwood said: " Nothing can be simpler than the art of the Hindu rosary, the Saiva rosary of 84 beads, and the Vaishnava of 108; but when you learn that the sacred number 84 (chaurāsi) is made up of the number of the 12 signs of the Zodiac, multiplied by the number of the 7 planets, and that the sacred number 108 is similarly made up, the moon being counted as three—the rising, full, and waning moon—instead of one, then you understand that the Hindu rosary symbolizes the whole circuit of the hosts of heaven.' Sir George Birdwood's concluding remark is particularly interesting: 'He was satisfied from the numbers of the beads strung on them, and their mode of division—in 12 groups of 7—that the earliest Christian rosaries . . . were originally derived from the rosaries of the Hindus.'

To return to our friend on the spikes. He has chosen a comfortable corner near the Ganges, but high up on the banks, and protected by walls and flagstones from the damp and wind. Overshadowing him is a sacred pipal-tree, on the trunk of which the pilgrims sprinkle the holy Ganges water. His cooking utensils are against the wall, and close by, on the wall and stones, is the fuel for fire; not sticks or coal or charcoal, but dried dung.

One can often see, not far away, a stone mortar and wooden pestle, for not a few of these holy men are confirmed bhang drinkers, and from the leaves of the hemp make their intoxicating beverage.

The sādhu's calf fears no prodigal's return: he is there to be adored, not to be devoured. To kill and eat a calf, and to make merry over it, would be an accumulation of horrors to the devout Hindu.

The picture of the sādhu's house was taken during a festival, when the people were celebrating the birth of Krishna. For the time the hut was turned into a temple, and contained gods and goddesses of all sizes and shapes and colours.

In this improvised temple you can see

THE SĀDHU'S WIFE.

[*Photo by Saeed Bros., Benares*

brass cups filled with Ganges water, also conch shells, and the collection plate.

The priestess—the sādhu's wife, we may hope—is reading a sacred book, and is ready to apply the coloured eye-earths to the faces of the prostrate worshippers. Meanwhile, her husband sits on the nails, receiving the adoration and alms of the people, and blessing the donors. Close by is a man with a withered arm. He had tied it to a bamboo, until the limb became rigid and useless.

Not far away is a sādhu who, to mortify the flesh, is seated in the midst of five fires. How far removed from this self-torture and 'colossal egoism' is the life to which we—and they—are called; a life pure, strong, helpful, industrious, animated by the spirit of Jesus Christ, 'who went about doing good.'

CHAPTER XII.

THE MOSLEMS.

ALTHOUGH Benares is famous as the citadel of Hinduism, out of its 220,000 inhabitants about 50,000 are Muhammadans, most of them being Sunnis ('traditionalists'). We have in this city not only fourteen or fifteen hundred temples, but some three or four hundred mosques as well. At least two of these mosques were built by the famous emperor Aurangzeb, on the ruins of Hindu temples which had been demolished by his orders.

Generally speaking, the Hindus and the Muhammadans live together in the same village or town without any bad feeling. Occasionally, when two of their religious festivals happen to clash, there may be trouble and even riot.

The Hindus are greatly distressed if they see or know that the Muhammadans are killing cows. The present Amir of Afghanistān being aware of this fact, ordered the Moslems of Delhi not to slaughter kine in his honour during his visit to India. But we must not think from this that no Hindu will ever take life or eat flesh. In Benares, many high-caste Hindus regularly eat fish. And in the villages round about, the high-caste people are delighted if they can get venison to eat. The goats and sheep sacrificed to the goddess Kāli are taken away and eaten by the worshippers. Perhaps the presence of the flesh-eating Muhammadans has helped to modify the practice of the Hindus in this matter.

The Moslems, as a rule, are not so well educated as the Hindus. They have not made such good use of the government schools and colleges as the Hindus have. But many of them are now beginning to find out the value of a Western education. It is strange but true, that only a small percentage of these people understand the Arabic prayers they offer. They learn some chapters from the Qurān, as a very clever parrot might. But generally speaking, they have no more idea than a gramophone what the words they are reciting signify. The learned men are not encouraged to translate the Qurān from the Arabic into the vernacular of the people. This is a pity, for if the people understood their own holy book, they would learn how often it testifies to Christ and the Christian's Bible.

These Moslems say that God (Allah) has 99 names. Some of these names are true and beautiful, but they do not include the best of all, the name of Father.

The Muhammadans believe that in order to be saved they must give alms to the poor, keep the great fast-days, pray five times a day, and go on pilgrimage to Mecca. Their creed in brief is, 'There is no god but Allah, and Muhammad is Allah's apostle.' The word for God, Allah, was the term used by the pagan Arabs for their chief god long before Muhammad was born. The Moslems believe in one god, but he is the deist's god rather than the god of the theists.

There are some true and beautiful things in the Qurān; but Muhammad taught nothing new. He got most of his ideas from the pagan Arabs, from the Jews, the Christians, the Zoroastrians and the Hanifs. (See, *The Original Sources of the Koran*, by Rev. W St. Clair Tisdall, M.A., D.D.)

The Moslems acknowledge that Muhammad died like any ordinary mortal. They say that Christ was taken to heaven without dying. We believe, of course, that Christ died before He ascended, but we are glad to know that the Muhammadans too confess that He is alive.

There are more than sixty million Moslems in India, the great majority of whom live in the north of the peninsula. We ought to do more to win these people for Christ.

Mr. Meredith Townsend says in *Asia and Europe*, when writing about Islam, that 'None who profess that faith ever quit it'; but this is not an accurate statement.

In 1893 the late Maulavi Imād-ud-Din, D.D., in a paper read at Chicago, presented a list of more than fifty Moslem converts, prominent in missionary work in India.

In our own mission at Faizabad, we have a convert who is a Hāfiz and a Hājji, that is to say, he knows the Qurān by heart, and has been on pilgrimage to Mecca. He came to know Christ through the testimony of the Qurān to the Christian revelation. Persecuted by his friends, he travelled from Bombay to Benares, and there in the bazaar met with our little band of preachers. By these he was instructed, and after submitting to severe tests was baptized. He is now one of the most trustworthy of our Indian Christian workers. We may, however, frankly confess that converts are seldom won from Islām. When every Hindu professes Christianity, the Church in India will then be faced by a problem of perhaps unique difficulty, the conversion of the Moslems. The fact is, that the Christian Church has not yet decided that these people need our gospel.

Their conception of God, which empha-

COURT OF AN EMPEROR'S PALACE.

sizes His unity and not His holiness, seems to have but little reformatory power. Their great prophet would not be tolerated in decent society to-day. And who but a Moslem would wish for his paradise? Islām is as inferior to Christianity as Muhammad is to Christ.

CHAPTER XIII

THE MOURNING OF THE SHI'AHS

ONCE more the Shi'ahs have commemorated the martyrdom of al-Husain, the son of 'Ali and the grandson of Muhammad.

In Morier's *Second Journey through Persia*, quoted by the Rev. T. P. Hughes, we have a most interesting account of the celebration of the Moharram in Persia, as witnessed by the 'Minister Plenipotentiary' in 1811. The sincerity of the Shi'ahs may be judged by Morier's description of the final scenes of the tragedy as performed in his presence.

'Al-Husain lay extended on the ground, ready to receive the death-stroke from a ruffian dressed in armour, who acted the part of executioner. At this moment a burst of lamentation issued from the multitude, and heavy sobs and real tears came from almost every one of those who were near enough to come under our inspection. The indignation of the populace wanted some object upon which to vent itself, and it fell upon those of the actors who had performed the part of Yazīd's soldiers. No sooner was al-Husain killed, than they were driven off the ground by a volley of stones, followed by shouts of abuse. We were informed that it is so difficult to procure performers to fill these characters, that on the present occasion a party of Russian prisoners were pressed into the army of Yazīd, and they made as speedy an exit after the catastrophe as it was in their power.'

The annual celebration of the death of Husain undoubtedly helps in some Indian cities to accentuate the differences between the Shi'ahs and the Sunnis; and the Deputy Commissioner congratulates himself if Moharram has passed off peacefully.

In Bombay, British artillery and infantry have been requisitioned to keep the excited crowds in order and to patrol the streets at night. The Wahhābis, who denounce the ta'ziahs (models of the mausoleum of Husain), and all such things as idolatrous, are often in danger of their lives during Moharram. When this festival occurs at the same time as the Holi, the authorities in certain towns know that, unless great care is taken, there may be serious disturbance. At Benares, about a century ago, these two festivals clashed. There was some street fighting in which the Muhammadans were defeated. They revenged themselves by retreating into the courtyard of Aurangzeb's mosque and broke down the Lāt of Shiva, which the Hindus held in high esteem. The Hindus pulled down a mosque, and then the military intervened.

Some years ago, the Hindus in a village not far from Lucknow discovered that a pipal-tree was in danger of being contaminated by the ta'ziahs which the Mohammedans wished to carry through the streets. Orders were issued by the Deputy Commissioner that the branches which might possibly be touched should be tied up safely out of reach.

But in some places, the Sunnis, Shi'ahs,

AURANGZEB'S MOSQUE.

and Hindus join together in the festival. At Benares this is the case, and the result of the prevailing harmony and catholicity is a general holiday.

Whisper it not in Persia, but the great day of the Moharram, on which the ta'ziahs are buried, is observed by many in Benares as the cockney observes Easter Bank-holiday at High Beech : of course, *mutatis mutandis*.

As some large ta'ziahs passed my house, we ran out with the camera to take a quick and secret picture. The people were crying out in the name of Husain, as they bore aloft the model of his tomb at Karbalā. One of the leaders noticed us. He hastened forward. What should we do ? Should we stand or run ? 'Would your honour,' he said, 'like me to stop the procession, that your honour may draw the picture with comfort ?'

We went to the place of burial. The roads were thick with dust and thronged with people. The walls and banks were covered with men, women and children, all in their Moharram 'best.' Here and there we met a company of men carrying long swords, which they flourished with great skill and no little pride, as they rushed rapidly to and fro. When the leader of one band noticed a Sahib at the back of the crowd, he, without much ceremony, pushed hither and thither the poor Muhammadans—who, quite unwittingly, were partially obscuring the view—in order that the Sahib might have the full benefit of the spectacle. If any of the young men had been less dexterous, front seats might have proved most disadvantageous.

We were now near to the burial ground, and saw merry-go-rounds, with mysteriously fashioned horses, hawkers of toys, and octopus-like phonographs which had glued themselves to the ears of Abdul Rahīm and his sons.

There was a booth, in front of which was an embossed picture of a lady who did nothing but roll her eyes. I do not know what was the attraction behind the gaily painted canvas. It was probably quite harmless.

As there were no burials going on, we

continued our walk round the fair. On a raised and covered platform, a maulavi was telling the story of Husain and his death. Acting on his suggestion, and probably not forgetting the reward, the men from time to time beat their breasts and lamented. A respectable young Muhammadan came up to me. He must have seen my camera. 'Would your honour like to take a photo of the people mourning?'

It was most kind of the young man, but the light was not good and we were not sure that the mourners would appreciate such attention. Some ta'ziahs were now buried. Holes were dug in the ground, and these were kept filled with water by the bihisties, who were well in evidence. The water is said to be in memory of Husain's dreadful thirst, just before he died. The smaller ta'ziahs, which are made of light cane and painted paper, were thrown into the holes and broken to pieces.

A small Hindu boy gave a pice to one of the bihisties. 'Yes,' said an old Muhammadan, who was standing close by, 'many

Hindus contribute, and if they give in the name of Hazrat Husain, on whom be peace, their sawāb (merit) will be great.'

In spite of the phonographs and swings, there is no doubt that the death of Husain means much to many of the Shi'ahs. They see in it something more than the 'natural result of a tribal feud.'

'How can I forget my people, seeing I am about to offer myself for their sakes?' said Husain as he started out on his last expedition. Listen to his dying prayer, as given in Pelly's translation: "O Lord, for the merit of me the dear child of the Prophet; O Lord . . . for the sake of young Abbās rolling in his blood . . .I pray Thee in the Day of Judgement, forgive, O merciful Lord, the sins of my grandfather's people, and grant me, bountifully, the key of the treasure of intercession."' Many hearts in Islam seem to have rebelled against the teaching that there is no intercession and no atonement. The Rev. W. St. Clair Tisdall informs us in *The Religion of the Crescent*, that 'The Shi'ahs generally believe that the deaths of Hasan and

Husain were propitiatory, and some at least among the Sunnis agree with them in asserting that the the martyred Husain died at Karbalā as their Redeemer.'

We may accept the suggestion, that the spirit of mildness and self-sacrifice shown in the life and death of Husain has made his memory live for centuries in the hearts of countless Shi'ahs.

CHAPTER XIV.

CASTE AT WORK.

A PLANTER in North India erected some houses for his coolies. He built them all in a row. One day, one of the coolies came with a complaint, 'The man who lives in the house next to mine lit a fire to-day. The smoke of his fire was driven by the wind and mingled with the smoke of my fire, and I am defiled, for he is a low-caste man!' 'I had to give him different quarters,' the planter informed me.

In a large city in the Punjab, an election for a new municipal councillor was held. A certain man was declared duly elected by a majority of votes. On the appointed day, all the councillors assembled to transact the business of the city. As soon as they saw the new councillor, they refused to sit in the same room with him. Why was that? Was he a drunkard, or a thief, or a wife-beater, was he unwashed or wearing filthy clothes? No: the

THE SWEEPER.

Photo by Rev. A. T. Cape]

SHIVA'S BULL.

[Photo by Rev. A. T. Cape

municipal councillors refused to sit in the same room with him, because he belonged to a low and despised caste! In India, a House of Parliament like ours, with men of different ranks of society and different occupations, all sitting together, and from time to time eating and drinking together, is absolutely unthinkable. Caste makes national unity impossible. Speaking generally, no man can 'break his birth's insidious bar' in India. If born in a 'log cabin,' he can never get to the 'White House.' If he starts in the 'tanyard,' he is a despised 'chamār,' and he must stop there. 'Let not the cobbler go beyond his last,' is a maxim rigorously enforced in India. He must stick to his bench and never aspire to the President's chair. And so India can never produce a William Carey.

One day some coolies were mending the walls of the mission compound, and on going to inspect the work, I noticed a goat sniffing at a heap of bricks. As the animal seemed profoundly interested in the pile, I put my hand on the top brick to see what was hidden. Immediately there was a terrible clamour among the coolies. Their food was on the ground covered by the bricks. The investigations of the goat were not resented, but as soon as an Englishman—unclean in their opinion—put his hand, not on the food, but on a brick some three feet distant, they considered their food defiled, and threw it away before my eyes!

A lady once saw a cobweb in her dining-room, so she called one of her servants and told him to get a long bamboo, fasten a few feathers to it, and then sweep away the cobweb. The man did as he was told without demur. But some servant had seen him and reported the matter. His caste-brethren held a committee meeting, and decided that the man should be punished for doing 'sweeper's' work, that is, the work of a man of a lower caste. When you know that his punishment was to feast his caste-brethren, you will not be surprised they brought him in guilty!

This incident will explain the necessity for keeping a number of servants in India.

Each man does the work his caste allows, and nothing else.

One day, in my own house, a low-caste man refused to lift a heavy piece of matting because a lower-caste man was touching it at the other end!

A missionary found a lad starving in a village in famine time. No one was helping him, and he was afraid to ask for help. He was a Hindu and they were Hindus, but he belonged to another village; he was a Brahman, and they were all low-caste folk.

An old man was dying on the banks of the Ganges. He was lying prone on the ground, weak with age and a dreadful disease. No one moved to help him. He was a man of high caste, and they feared to approach him. He might have cursed them had they touched him. 'Who is my neighbour?' asks the Hindu, and his religion replies, 'The man of your caste, he is your neighbour.'

May the Spirit of Jesus Christ speedily abolish the caste spirit, so that the millions of India may rejoice in the comfort and strength of a common Brotherhood!

CHAPTER XV.

THE SACRED BULL.

WHEN the grass is long and fresh and the kitchen garden green, then he comes. When the gate is open, he walks through; when the gate is closed, he climbs over the low mud-wall. Sometimes he will come on a moonlight night in the hot weather, when you are sleeping out of doors. If he visits you then, you may wake up in a fright, for he is a big beast, with a big hump on his shoulder and with big eyes.

It is not an easy thing to get him out of the compound. He will run round and round and miss the gate every time! If he charges, then you must do the running. If he damages your garden and endangers your life, you must not shoot him, for he is a sacred animal. But you may do anything short of taking his life. It is a serious matter to be born a cow or a bull

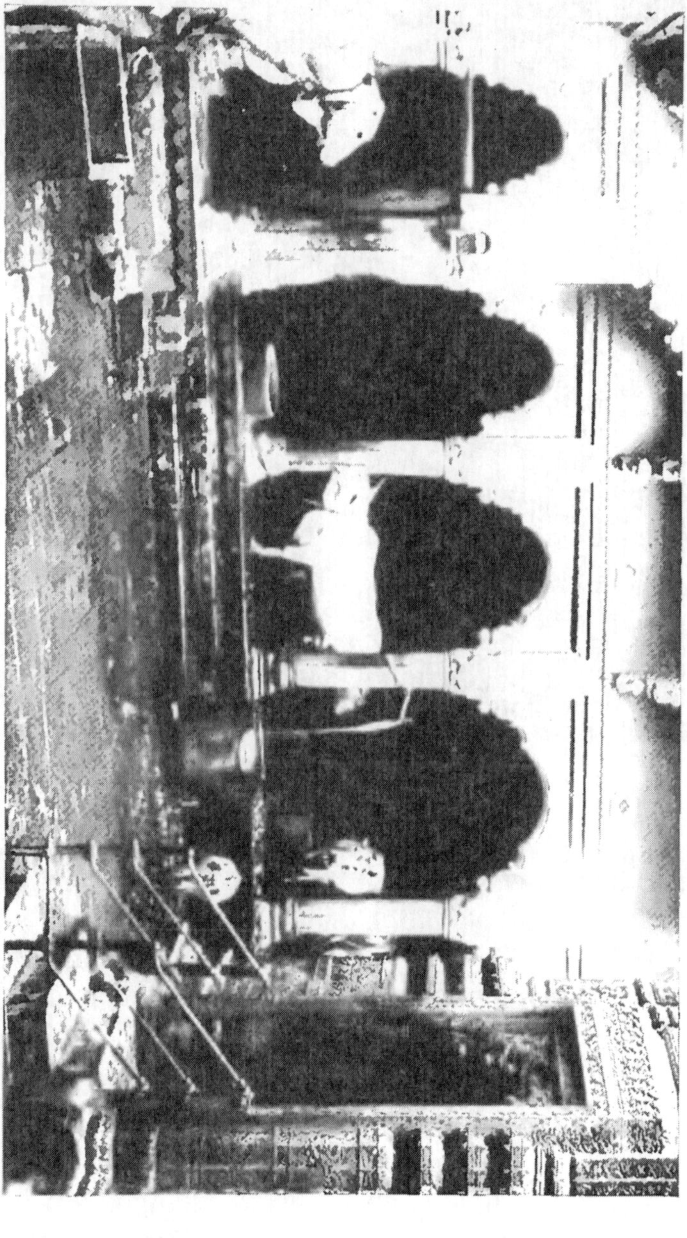

SOME SACRED BULLS. [*Photo by Saeed Bros., Benares*

in India. If one of these animals should trespass into a farmer's field and damage the crops, the farmer will not kill it, he will be content to fracture one of its limbs. Should a bullock fall and be unable to rise of itself, the owner comes to its help. He lights a straw fire underneath it. If closer examination reveals the fact that a leg is broken, the farmer respects the beast too much to put it out of its agony. He leaves it alone with hunger and thirst and the crows and the jackals.

Thousands of years ago, the Hindus were accustomed to kill and eat the cow, to commemorate the advent of a distinguished visitor. Now they would consider such an act as the worst of crimes.

They believe that a cow's tail can ferry them over the river of death, and many a criminal has died in peace because he has received permission to grasp a cow's tail before the lever was pulled.

The sacred bull is quite a common object in Benares. When a man is dead, then is the time to do what you can to show your love for him, many Hindus think. So what they do is this: they go to a farmer and buy a young bull, then they send for the priests, and the priests sprinkle holy water over the animal in the name of the dead man. They also offer a fire sacrifice in the temple. Then the bull, after being married to four young cows, is allowed to wander wherever he likes. He likes the bazaars, where he can sample the grain and the vegetables. He likes the farmers' crops. Sometimes, as I have already said, he likes our garden.

But how does this wandering bull benefit the dead man? Well, you see, he is sacred to the great god Shiva. And the great god Shiva is said to be highly delighted when a bull is set free to enjoy himself, without being compelled to draw a cart, or thresh the corn. So the great god Shiva says to Yama the god of the infernal regions, 'Put so much "merit" to that man's credit,' and when they come to add it all up and to strike the balance, they find that the dead man got so much "merit" by means of the bull, that he is entitled to immediate release!

CHAPTER XVI.

MOSQUITOES AND FLEAS.

THESE we have always with us. In the Rains other creatures come as well. If we have our dinner on the verandah, because of the heat, the insects quickly discern our presence and then they all come.

'Flies get entry into your mouth, into your eyes, into your nose; you eat flies, drink flies, and breathe flies. Lizards, cockroaches, and snakes get into the bed, ants eat up the books; scorpions sting you on the foot. Everything bites, stings, or bruises. An insect with eleven legs is swimming in your tea-cup, a nondescript with nine wings is struggling in the small beer, and a caterpillar with several dozen eyes in his belly is hastening over the bread-and-butter. All nature is alive, and seems to be gathering all her entomological hosts to eat you up!' From which description we may judge that Sydney Smith knew more about insects in the tropics than he did about the work of Indian missionaries or English Methodism.

But to return to our mosquitoes. They are a source of annoyance and danger to all whom they attack. The pain of their bite is not great, but considerable enough to be undesirable.

Our chief complaint against the mosquito is that it, or rather she, spreads the dreaded malarial fever. Not all the mosquitoes do this, but only those that belong to the Anopheles species. And this is the way it is done. When she bites a person who has the fever, the poison germ is drawn in with the blood she drinks. Inside the mosquito's body, the parasite changes its form and works its way to the insect's 'front-feeder,' and when the mosquito bites another person, then the poison germ gets its opportunity, and transfers itself to the healthy man. If enough poison is put into this man, he will have malarial fever.

Now there are several ways of preventing this sickness. One is to kill the mosquitoes whenever you see them. Another way and a better is to destroy their larvae. This can be done by pouring paraffin oil on the ponds where they breed. If possible all ponds and stagnant water near houses should be drained off. If there are still many mosquitoes left, you can protect yourself by sleeping on beds with mosquito curtains.

But if in spite of all your precautions you get bitten, then you can take quinine, which has the power to kill the poison germ in the blood.

Now we come to the flea. This we fear almost more than the mosquito. And for this reason, that doctors tell us that the flea can give you the dreadful plague.

Suppose—as is very likely in India—there are some rats in a man's house. Well, these rats get the plague. These rats have fleas which bite them and imbibe the poison. When the rat dies of the plague, the flea leaves the cold, dead body and turns its attention to man. If it now bites him, he may get the plague, and if he gets the plague he is nearly sure to die. In the big cities in India, the sanitary officials are doing all they can to catch and kill the rats.

It is very sad to think that many people in India say that the British government is spreading the plague to reduce the population. Some wicked men tell this to the ignorant villagers to make them dissatisfied with their rulers.

People have a much better chance of escaping from this terrible disease by consenting to be inoculated. And this inoculation the government doctors are willing to perform free of charge.

'It has been established beyond doubt that inoculation is a most valuable protective against plague, and even when it does not afford immunity, it doubles the chances of recovery.' Such is the publicly expressed opinion of the present Viceroy of India.

The chief means of combating the plague are: the destruction of rats, the evacuation of infected villages, and the inoculation of the people. But these three methods cost money, and this is not always forthcoming; and unfortunately, those most concerned, the people themselves, seem sometimes least concerned. Without the willing and intelligent co-operation of the people, the government can do little. And so the rat flea wins.

As you are told elsewhere, in one week, in the year 1907, eighty-two thousand people in India died of plague. If this awful fact is seriously considered, we shall be able to join with the King-Emperor when he says to the Viceroy, 'I am deeply moved when I think of the misery that has been borne with such silent patience in all those stricken homes. . . . It is my earnest hope and prayer that further measures, now being prepared by your Excellency in consultation with zealous and able officers, may be crowned with merciful success.'

CHAPTER XVII.

THE NĪM-TREE.

THIS is one of the specially sacred trees of India. Some people say the goddess of small-pox (Sītalā) lives in it. Others will tell you that all the gods and goddesses reside there. When you know how useful the Nīm is, you will not be surprised that the Indians think very highly of it.

Here is a detailed list of the various uses of this 'cure-all.'

Poultices are made from the boughs and applied to wounds and sores.

The leaves can be eaten to purify the blood.

The oil taken from the tree is efficacious in healing wounds.

The inner bark is steeped in cold water and then is well boiled. The liquid thus obtained is most useful in curing fever.

The root, bark, leaf, fruit and flower

are all ground together and then taken as a powder. This is said to be a cure for leprosy.

The flowers are cooked in clarified butter and eaten with spices.

People who sleep in the shade of the Nīm will never have fever—so they say. A twig of this tree is used as a tooth-brush. The soft bark is torn back, the wood is ground into pulp and the teeth are then cleaned with it. Then the tooth-brush is thrown away. You can buy about fifty twigs for a farthing, if you haven't a tree of your own. Some people think that a small-pox patient can be cured by fanning him with the leaves of this tree! Others say that the snake-bite can be cured in this way!

Your neighbour cannot tell you a lie while he stands beneath the Nīm. Once a magistrate wanted to plant a number of Nīm-trees in the centre of a small market town to protect the people from the heat. But when the merchants of the place heard of this, they went to the magistrate and said: 'Nourisher of the poor ! Be pleased to refrain from showing your goodness in this way ; if the Nīm-trees are planted, our town will be ruined and our livelihood destroyed, for standing under a Nīm-tree who will be able to buy and sell his goods ? '

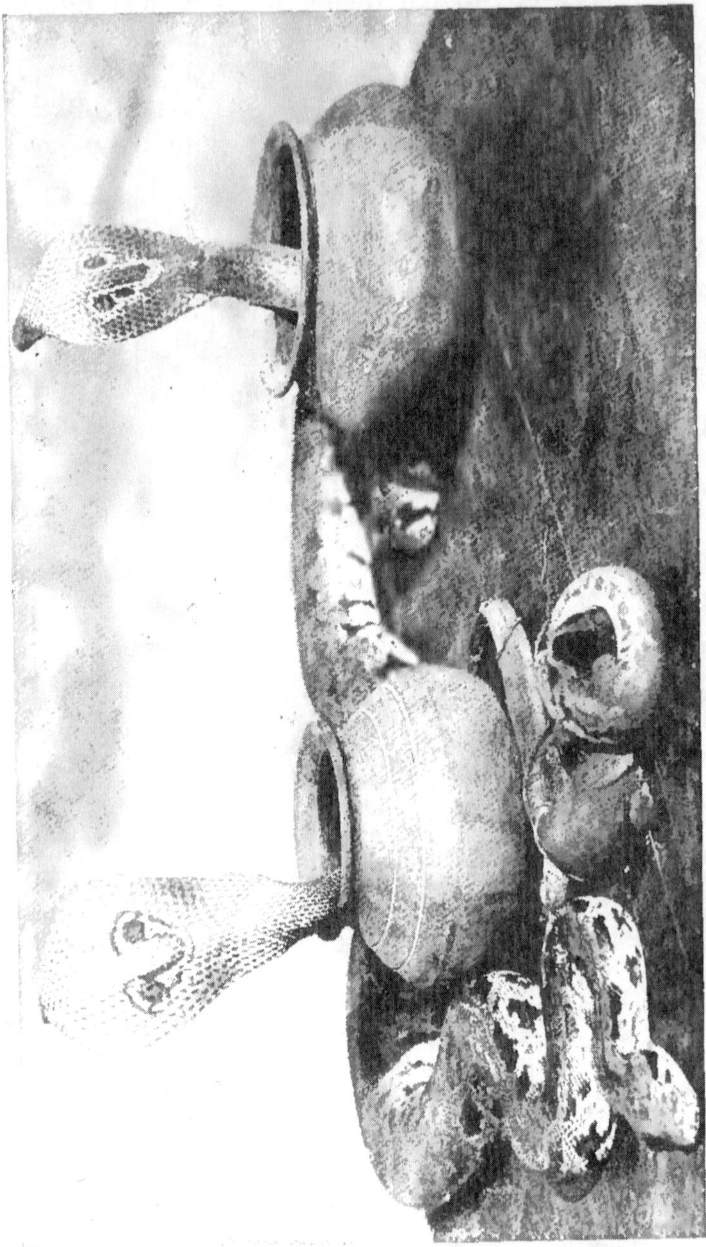

POTTED COBRAS!

[*Photo by Saeed Bros., Benares*

CHAPTER XVIII.

SNAKES.

Boys often ask if we have any snakes in India. Yes, we have. There are two hundred and thirteen species of snakes in this country. But fortunately only thirty-three species are poisonous. The deadly snakes have two teeth in the upper jaw, and these are the grooved, erectile poison-fangs. A poisonous snake makes two marks (:) in the flesh when it bites. The non-poisonous reptile makes more than two (: : :).

Perhaps you would like to know what can be done to save the life of a man who has been bitten by a deadly snake. A bandage should be tied at once above the wound. Then the bitten place should be lanced so that the blood may flow freely. Sometimes it is wise to apply a red-hot iron to the wound, or some acid. The patient should be kept in the fresh air.

Thousands of people in India die every year of snake-bite. If the patient lives in a village, as he probably does, his friends send for some sorcerer, who tries to cure him by incantations. These are, of course, of no use whatever. Good doctors are very scarce in India, and the poor village people have often no one who can help them at such times.

Many thousands of Hindus worship snakes, and therefore refuse to kill them. There are special shrines for snake-gods in the Himalayan Mountains. In Benares, Nāgīswar is the serpent deity, and Nāg Kuān, a very deep well, is one of the oldest shrines in the city.

You may wonder why the Hindus worship snakes. Well, you see, first of all they fear them because of their deadly poison. Then they notice that some of the snakes are harmless, and seem to like to live with the people. These they would come to regard as the ghosts of their ancestors, and guardians of their houses and goods. Then, again, some worship them because they are an emblem of life and eternity. The people would notice that the snake renews his life and is very long-lived. Perhaps these are some of the reasons why Indians reverence snakes.

It is said in India, that if a man dies without having a son to inherit his house and treasures, he will return to the house in the form of a snake, and will look after the treasure himself!

Many villagers believe in the 'Domunha,' a snake with a mouth at both ends; but though there is certainly a snake which has a tail as thick as its head, I have never yet been able to discover a 'Domunha.'

There is a very peculiar creature called the Biskhapra, or poison-head. It looks something like a large and very ugly lizard. It is probably an iguana. But all the villagers say that it is the most deadly of all snakes, so deadly in fact, that it can dispense with poison fangs! In spite of its bad looks and its worse reputation, it is really quite harmless.

But let us get back to snakes proper.

One day, my little terrier dog began to wail as if terribly frightened. The study door was opened, and there I saw a huge cobra ready to strike. I took down the gun and shot the reptile's head right off, but its long black body kept on wriggling for nearly two hours.

The cobra's bite is peculiarly deadly. It is interesting to know that one cobra cannot poison another by its venomous injections. But if the cobra had bitten me, I should probably have been dead within a few hours.

Once when sleeping in the garden, the watchman cried out, 'Wake up, sir, wake up! there is a big snake close by, and it has bitten one of the fowls.' Within ten minutes the hen was dead. She had been killed while defending her little ones from the attacks of the snake.

These horrid reptiles sometimes get into our house. We soon form the habit of never putting on a boot or shoe without first shaking it to see if there is a snake inside. If there should happen to be a small frog wedged up in the toe, you get

A YOUNG SNAKE-CHARMER.

[*Photo by Saeed Bros., Benares*

such a fright when you put your foot in!

We often have snake-charmers come round to our house. They profess to be able to cure the bites of poisonous snakes, with the bark of certain trees.

The peculiar music of the gourd has a wonderful effect upon the cobras. It is most interesting to watch 'some chattering snake-tamer . . . charm the hooded death to angry dance to drone of beaded gourd.'

The snake-charmer often brings with him a bottle of scorpions, which he will empty into your hand—if you are willing.

The bite of a full-grown scorpion which has been resting for a while and generating plenty of poison, is agonizing in the extreme.

The snake-man sometimes brings with him a mongoose, a ferret-like creature which is the snake's deadly enemy.

One day a snake-charmer brought in a mongoose which he had caught in our garden while it was fighting with a cobra. You will understand that we are glad to know that quite a small colony of mongoose resides in our compound. The combat between these two deadly enemies is most exciting. From side to side they sway, backwards and forwards they move, sometimes the mongoose will bound right over his foe; then, at the right moment—and the mongoose knows when that has come—a lightning-like leap and the snake's head is between the jaws of its adversary, who shakes it as a terrier does a rat.

The mongoose can be tamed and kept as a pet, but it is an incorrigible thief.

A BENARES PUBLIC-HOUSE.

[*Photo by C. P. Cape*

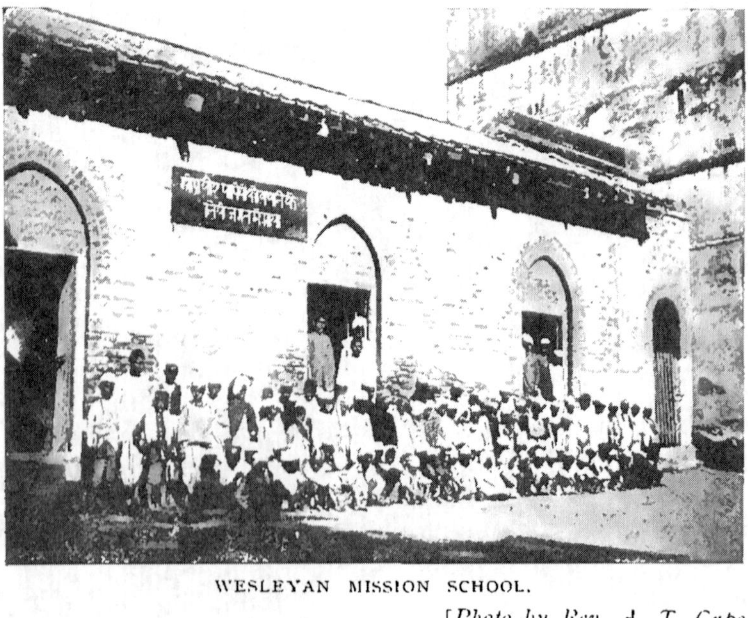

WESLEYAN MISSION SCHOOL.

[*Photo by Rev. A. T. Cape*

CHAPTER XIX.

A BENARES PUBLIC-HOUSE.

GENERALLY speaking, the people of India are not intemperate. Many millions of Hindus, as well as the Moslems, never touch alcohol. But a drunken Hindu is not an uncommon sight in Benares. Many of the low-castes drink, and drink heavily, and some of the educated Indians are learning to drink English wines and spirits. This is a very great pity, for it seems to be much harder for an Indian to drink in moderation than for an Englishman.

The Benares public-house is very uninviting to Western eyes. A dirty, disreputable cattle-shed—that is what it looks like. Visit it at about 8.30 in the evening, and you will see groups of men, women, and children, sitting about on the mud floor, drinking the 'sharāb' out of small earthen pots, which are thrown away and broken as soon as empty. The publican tells me that the average man can get drunk for sixpence. Even when that stage is reached, the law allows him to be supplied with drink.

For the privilege and monopoly of dispensing this villanous stuff for one year, the publican pays the government four hundred pounds. As the licence is put up to auction and is sold to the highest bidder, you will understand that the purchaser is sorely tempted to adulterate the liquor he dispenses, and so recoup himself for the large sum spent to obtain the license. You will notice, in the front of the photograph, an elderly man with a beard. He happened to be standing near the public-house when the picture was taken, and great was his horror when he realized that he, a Muhammadan, had been caught so close to a drink-shop! Moslems can occasionally be discovered inside these disgusting places; yes, and Christians too The man with the long hair is one of India's 'saints.' He had only gone to the public-house to beg, we were told.

Unfortunately statistics and other facts show that the drinking habit is spreading in India. There has been an extraordinary increase in the consumption of alcoholic liquors in recent years.

God save India from England's curse! And may all who are in authority be shown what they ought to do, to—in the words of the Secretary of State for India—'prevent the spread of this dire, new, additional plague.'

CHAPTER XX.

MARRIAGE.

PLEASE imagine that you are a little Brahman girl of Benares. You are six years old. Your father and mother think it is quite time you were married. So they send for the barber and the family priest and tell them their wish. They also add that in the house of Gopi Nāth there is a boy of about eight years old, who, they think, would make you a suitable husband. So the barber and the priest call on Gopi Nāth and tell him what your parents desire. Then Gopi Nāth's family priest asks for your 'janam-pattri,' that is the paper on which are recorded the year, lunar day, configuration and relative position of the planets of your birth. This is compared with the 'janam-pattri' of Gopi Nāth's son. If the horoscope shows that the boy's stars are 'stronger' than

A WORSHIPPER OF SHIVA.

[*Photo by Saced Bros., Benares*

yours, all will be well and you will be able to marry him. The priests decide that all is in order, and that you can marry. But before the marriage comes the betrothal. The boy must send you some presents—clothes, sweets, money, toys, and things of that sort. Then you or your parents must send him some presents in return; and your father must go to the boy's house and make a red mark on his forehead. That is a sort of seal to the contract.

Not very long after this you will be married. The month and the day will be decided by the family priests. It must be in February, March, April, May, June or November. Then your father will have to send a 'lagan,' that is, a letter stating the day of marriage, to the father of the bridegroom. As soon as he gets this message, he will issue invitations to the wedding, and he will get a number of horses and elephants—if he can afford them—and a lot of men to play drums and trumpets, and some to fire off muskets and generally to make as much noise as they can. Some of the guests will come on their horses and some in carriages and others on foot. When the procession gets near to the house, a lot of fireworks will be let off. Then your friends will say, 'Behold the bridegroom cometh, let us go forth to meet him.' But before your friends go forth to meet the bridegroom, a barber will be sent to you with a rupee and some rice in a little earthen pot. The barber will have some sweets given to him and then he must return to the wedding procession. As soon as the bridegroom gets quite close to your house, your father will have to go to meet him. Then your door will be covered over with cow-dung to purify it, and keep off spirits. Your father must then put a mark on the boy's forehead and a garland round his neck and must also touch his feet. He will also have to give him some presents—rupees, clothes, horses, and so on, according to his ability. Then the bridegroom must retire for a while into a separate house, or he can rest under some trees and amuse himself and his friends with music and dancing.

A sort of shed will be made for the wedding ceremony, kept up by five props. This will be in the courtyard of your house. Then the bridegroom and his friends come in and your father must receive him and wash his feet.

After that the bridegroom is given something to eat, upon which a priest has asked a blessing. Your father will cover you with a piece of yellow cloth, while another piece is tied to the bridegroom. Then the god Ganesha is worshipped so that he may bring you good luck. Then the bridegroom's father's family priest repeats the names of the bridegroom's male ancestors, and your family priest repeats the names of your ancestors. You will have to put your hand into the boy's right hand. Then comes an important moment when one of your garments is fastened with a knot to the bridegroom's shawl. After that you have to sit down on the right of the boy, both facing the east, and the priest will recite the names of some of the great gods. Now is the time to give the priest his fee.

Then an altar is built and the priest burns incense on it. The gods are worshipped, and gifts made to the priests.

When that is over, some one will cover you both with a sheet. Then your brother will give some rice to the boy, who will give you some of it, which you must put on a flat stone.

After that, your father puts your hand into the hand of the bridegroom and you both have to walk round the fire in which incense is burned; at the same time the priest makes seven little heaps out of the rice you put on the stone.

You are now married. Then your priest gives your young husband an address, in which he says that he must always take his wife with him when he goes on pilgrimage and to the temples; he must be true to her always and must not leave her when in trouble. The priest is really speaking for you, the young wife, and says at the end, 'Vishnu and Agni and the Brahmans are witnesses between us.'

Your husband replies, 'I will do what my bride asks; but my wife must love, honour, and obey me, and must be with me in all my troubles.' Then you will have to say, 'I promise to do as you ask. Vishnu, Fire, and the Brahmans witness between us both.'

While the priest is praying, the bridegroom will sprinkle some water over your head, and you must both worship the Sun.

This done, the bridegroom will put his hand on your heart and some coloured powder on the parting in your hair. He then puts his shoes on your feet, but removes them immediately.

Your husband now leaves you, and you do not see him again till you are about twelve years old. When that time comes you must say good-bye to your mother and go with your husband to live with him.

If your boy husband should die, the people will call you a widow—even if you are only eight years old! They will shave off your hair and take away your ornaments—but you ought not to be troubled with such thoughts now. May you be very happy! May the evil of every hour remain far from you!

It has occurred to me that perhaps English girls would like to know if the Indian girls are pretty. I don't think I can do better than translate a few lines from a book called the Prem Sāgar, and then you can judge for yourselves.

'O great prince, when the girl was twelve years old, then having seen the radiance of her moon-like face, the full-moon became emaciated; before the blackness of her hair, the darkness of the night of the new moon began to be pale; having seen the tapering of her braided hair, the female snake having left its skin, disappeared; having observed the bending of her eyebrows, the rainbow began to palpitate; having perceived the largeness and playfulness of her eyes, the deer, fish, and the spotted fork-tail were abashed; having seen the beauty of her nose, the sesamum flower faded away; having perceived the redness of her lips, the bright-red gourd of the bimba began to lament; having observed the rows of her teeth, the heart of the pomegranate was torn; having noticed the softness of her cheeks, the rose abstained from blossoming ; having seen the roundness of her neck, the doves began to flutter ; having perceived the slenderness of her waist the lion lived the life of a hermit ; looking at the smoothness of her skin, the banana ate camphor ; having perceived the fairness of her body, gold was ashamed, and the yellow flower of the champa blushed ; in comparison with her hands and feet, the lotus had no dignity. Thus the elephant gaited, cuckoo-voiced one . . . who robbed all these of their beauty.'

Now you know what beauty is, in the eyes of an Indian !

As some of you may be interested to know how such a beautiful girl would be dressed, I will give you the description as translated from the Prem Sāgar, by Mr. F. Pincott :

'Subsequently, one day, that fresh maiden having applied sweet-scented unguents, and washed away with pure water every impurity, and combed her hair, and arranged the parting, and filled in the division with pearls, and had used collyrium and tooth-powder, and applied henna and cochineal, and eaten betel, and having sent for excellent jewel-studded golden ornaments, and arranged herself in head-decorations, forehead pendants, forehead circlet, a forehead band, an ear-knot, earrings, four-pearl ear ornaments, pearl earrings, a nose-ring of large pearls, a gold patch on the nose-ring, with pendants, a neck-brooch threaded on a necklace of two rows of pearls, a moon-necklace, a gold and coral necklace, a five-stringed necklace, a seven-stringed necklet, a neck ornament on the throat itself, armlets, nine-gemmed bracelets, bangles, wristlets, bracelets, rings, signets, seals, toe-rings, girdles of bells, anklets of sorts, footlets, great toe rings, and toe ornaments; and arranged herself in a clean, glittering wide petticoat with a border of real pearls, and a brilliant dress with a border and a hem, and a splendid bodice, close-fitting, and over that a glittering veil, and having furthermore perfumed herself . . . . she went out.'

THE BIHISTI.

Photo by C. P. Cape]

THE HINDU WATER-MAN.

[*Photo by C. P. Cape*

CHAPTER XXI.

OUR WATER SUPPLY.

As we have no water laid on in the house, it is necessary to send to the well or the stand-pipe for it. At the stand-pipe we get Ganges water, and this is what we generally use. A visit to the Ganges at Benares is enough to make the strongest temperance advocate waver in his faith. City sewers, dead dogs, dead men pollute the river. But our water is pumped up on the safe side of the city, and it is properly filtered at the water-works before it comes to us. There are two sorts of water-men here: one is a Moslem and he carries the water in a skin; the other is a caste Hindu. The Moslem servant is called a 'bihisti,' that is, a heavenly-man, as a carrier of water in a dry and thirsty land deserves to be called. He has to pay about 6s. 8d. for the goat-skin in which he carries the water. One skin will last him for about six months. Our 'bihisti' often wears a khākī coat which he bought from a soldier. I suppose you know that khākī is a Hindustani word, and that it means dust-coloured. Some Hindu ascetics who cover themselves with dust are called 'khākī.' A humble man is 'khāk-sar,' that is, a 'like-dust' man. Well, this water-man carries his water-skin about with him, and when it cracks, he mends it himself. Now no caste Hindu would dream of doing that. To carry and to pierce an animal's skin would be abhorrent to him. So the Hindu water-man here carries the water in tins. These are old empty kerosene oil-tins. The empty oil-tins are much desired by the people. From them they can make water-tins, water-pots, flower-pots, bird-cages, portmanteaus, and many other useful articles.

It is a great convenience to be able to get water from the stand-pipes. It is not easy to keep the well-water clean, for when the people bathe, the water they have used runs back into the well. The new wells are now so built that the dirty water must flow away and so cannot pollute the clean.

Our well is very old and deep. You will be sorry to know that every year quite a number of people, generally women, commit suicide by jumping into one of their deep, dark village wells.

When the water-works were first opened, the people of Benares said they could not use the water, as it came through pipes which had been made and erected by the unclean hands of Europeans and Moslems. But they were told that the Ganges water was so holy that in its flowing it cleansed away all impurities. And this wonderful discovery reconciled the people to the use of the pipe-water.

When the engineers began to build a bridge over the Ganges at Benares, many of the Hindus said that the river goddess would not consent to be bridged. And they were not a little delighted to hear that the engineers were experiencing considerable difficulty in obtaining a reliable foundation for one of the piers.

When at last the bridge was ready, some of the Hindus said that it would be sacrilege to use it, as they would be walking over a goddess, Mother Ganges. When the utility of the new bridge was realized, it was decided that they could use it—if they took their shoes off! They now cross the bridge with their shoes on, unless they happen to belong to a class of Hindus who nearly always carry their shoes, to ease their feet and to save the leather.

PLAGUE PATIENTS. [Photo by *Clifton & Co., Bombay*

CHAPTER XXII.

THE PLAGUE.

We can well remember when it visited us. Returning from an out-station, we were told that Patras, the brightest boy in our orphanage, was in hospital with the plague. The hospital was a little hut of straw and bamboo. You must understand that very few people recover if they are attacked by the plague. When they are ill they are put into a well-ventilated hut, and when they die, their bodies, and the hut, and the bed, and the clothes are all burnt, to prevent infection. Patras was visited daily. Two English doctors did their best for the lad, and the doctors in India are brave, clever men.

On the Wednesday, Patras saw a piece of white paper by his bed; he picked it up and said, 'Through Jesus Christ my heart has been made clean like this.'

On the Thursday he rallied, and our hopes revived. On the Friday morning he got worse, and in the evening, while our soldiers' prayer-meeting was being held, a little orphan boy came running in, and cried out, 'Sir, Patras is dead.'

The next morning we buried him. The undertaker would not help because the lad had died of plague. The coffin was very heavy, the lid did not fit. . . . Not long before he died, he began to sing in Urdū, his mother tongue, a hymn which begins :—

> O sick ones, be comforted,
> The Lord is now approaching.

The lad knew, and not long after, the Lord whom he loved came into the plague hut, and took our orphan boy away to that land where there is no famine and no plague and no orphans, and where never a grave is dug.

Patras was a 'full' member, and on the Sunday he had stayed for the Lord's Supper.

As one thinks of Patras, of his testimony in life and death, one feels that money spent on orphanage work is money well expended.

While the brother of Patras was in the segregation camp, he heard the people say, 'There is a Christian in that hut yonder: he has the plague. Let us see if the English doctors will poison him, as they have killed our friends. Perhaps, as he is a Christian, they will spare his life. If they do, something may happen to the doctors, for we shall know then for certain that he has killed our friends.' When Patras died, they said, 'Although he was a Christian, he was a Hindustāni too, so the doctors poisoned him also.'

The Monday after we lost our orphan boy, the orderly came in haste to report that one of the Wesleyans of the South Staffordshire Regiment was ill with plague. We rode off at once to the hospital, and saw a tent pitched just outside. 'You can't go in, sir,' said the assistant-surgeon, 'it's a case of plague.'

'I know that,' I replied, 'but I'm the chaplain.' He would not grant permission to enter without the consent of the senior medical officer

'I've no objection, if you haven't,' was his reply. We spoke to the sick man about Christ, and we spoke plainly.

For four days he was visited. On the Friday a note came from the hospital to say that the lad was dying. We went at once, but the soldier-lad was dead. The same day, the buglers sounded the 'Last Post' over his grave.

I met the orderly a few days after. 'He got worse suddenly, sir. "I'm feeling cold, hold my hand," he said, just before he died. He tried to sing a hymn, sir, last night, something about angels. I didn't know what it was, or I'd have given him a lift with it. He thought some one was calling him. "Who's calling me?" he cried out all of a sudden. "No one's calling you," I told him. But I knew then, sir, that he was going.'

One Friday we were visiting a missionary. His daughter, a bright, sweet little maid about eight years old, was playing with her dollies in the room close by. The father and mother were sad because their little one was about to leave them for

England, where she would have to spend many years of her life, far away from those who loved her most. She was to sail from Bombay in eight days' time. On the following Monday we heard that she had the plague. On the Tuesday morning came a note from the father asking us to pray that she might not die. She died at noon. One hour later she was in her grave.

Please pray for the missionaries' wives and children; yes, and for all European women and children in India.

I have only told you of three deaths through plague. You will not forget that in one week there were 82,000.

CHAPTER XXIII.

THE WOMEN AND GIRLS.

THE Hindu women and girls of this part of India are very ignorant. If you put 10,000 of them into the Albert Hall, London, and gave each one a copy of the New Testament in her own mother tongue, 9,985 would be unable to read the book. Not many of the men and boys can write, only 578 out of every 10,000. One reason why the people are so backward is that in India, only certain classes have been expected to be educated. It has been considered quite a mistake and sometimes a sin to teach the girls. Beside this, the girls are expected to work in the fields, or to mind the baby while others work. The government is now opening free schools all over the provinces, and it is hoped that many more people will

A LITTLE MOTHER

Photo by Rev. A. T. Cape]

THE BOY WHO DIED OF THE PLAGUE.

(Patra is sitting in the front row on the left of the group).

[*Photo by C. P. Cape*

be able to read and write in a few years' time.

Some of the priests of Benares do not want to have the women and the girls taught. 'They love the darkness rather than the light, because their deeds are evil.'

It is very difficult for the missionaries to train the girls, because they marry when they are about twelve, and then have to leave school. The girls must then be taught in their own homes, and in the city of Benares there are not a few who are being instructed in this way.

Some of these girls are widows, and some of these widows are very sad. Less than a hundred years ago many of the widows were allowed to burn themselves alive with their husband's corpse. When the missionaries and others tried to stop this great cruelty, many of the Hindus were very angry and asked that they might be allowed to retain the privilege of roasting their widowed mothers alive! The women who died in this way were called 'sati,' that is, faithful. We have never read of a man showing his love for his dead wife by being willing to be burnt alive with her dead body!

Although the British government has stopped this horrible custom, it is to be feared that many of the twenty-six million widows of India are very unhappy. This is what an Indian has said on this matter: 'Imagine yourself a Hindu widow at the age of ten, most orthodox of educated Indians. Imagine the shame, the misery, the isolation, the utter hopelessness of her life. And tell us if you really believe that you who tolerate it, and you who enforce it, on your daughter or sister, can congratulate yourself on that passionate love of your fellow creatures which constitutes true patriotism. . . . The abolition of sati initiated a movement of mercy in favour of Hindu widows which cannot attain its full fruition till the iniquitous custom of enforced widowhood receives its death-blow at the hands of an enlightened and humanized public opinion. Much better burn the widows than subject them to the cruelty and shame of having

MINDING BABY.

A SUTTEE STONE.

THREE VILLAGE MAIDENS.

their heads shaven, their meals restricted, and their very presence regarded as inauspicious.'

When Sir Frederick Treves was in Benares and saw the marigolds and jasmine which had been offered to the gods, dirty with the filth of the lanes and temples, he called Benares 'a city of trampled flowers.' India is a country of trampled flowers. The Zanana system is cruel both to the men and women. For without the influence of the women in social life, the men suffer and the nation suffers. And in some Zananas even the women, the mothers of the coming India, harbour defiling thoughts. One must be silent. But some of us know: 'Lilies that fester smell far worse than weeds.'

Help us to save the white flowers for Christ.

To comfort and to bless these poor wives and widows, Christian women go to their homes and teach them to read, and tell them about the Lord Jesus. But as the Christian workers in India are so few, not very many of these sad hearts can know the comforting Christ. You can help your Indian sisters by assisting the Zanana and Girls' school work of our Missionary Society. You can pray, you can collect money, and perhaps some day you yourself will come to India to tell the glad tidings of God's love in Christ.

CHAPTER XXIV.

A VILLAGE SCHOOL.

It resembles a cattle-shed, only it has no windows. But it has one door, so that a limited amount of light and air can enter the school. It is very much like the houses round about. The Hindu believes in many things, but he does not believe in fresh air and sunlight. So he shuts them out—and lets in the plague. It would be a good thing to make at least one window in our school, but the room does not belong to us. It is owned by a high-caste Hindu who doesn't like windows, because he has a wife and daughters who must be kept as invisible as possible. There are no benches or seats or black-boards or desks in the school. The only piece of furniture is the master's stick. He refrains from using it when he is asleep. A new scholar is brought by his father, who addresses the teacher as follows: 'I hand you this boy to be taught; his flesh is yours, but his bones are mine.'

If the stick should not be handy when a mistake in an addition sum is discovered, the teacher does what he can to pull an ear from the boy's head.

There are only a few slates in the school, and yet every scholar can learn to write. There is one thing in the Indian village you can get cheap—that is dust. It is plentifully sprinkled on the school-floor, and instead of pens or pencils, the boys use their fingers. A few of the farmers' sons can afford slates and pens and ink. The slates are wood, and the ink is chalk and water. The pens are peculiar. The first time I had one, I was a little alarmed, for it was about six feet long. But my munshi took it in hand and cut it into twelve parts. You buy these pens by the yard and not by the dozen, as in England. He then took one of the twelve pieces, and sharpened one end with a knife, till it resembled a quill pen. Having cut the point of the pen obliquely he handed me the finished article. Then I began at the end of the book, and wrote from right to left. Only a few of our village boys can afford to use the pen and slate. We pay the Hindu teacher six shillings and eightpence a month, and he provides his own board and lodging. The lads learn to read and write Hindi, and to do sums in their heads and on the ground. Our evangelist teaches them hymns, the catechism, and the Gospels. He is also supposed to direct the activities of the Hindu teacher.

CHAPTER XXV

INDIAN MELAS.

A MELA is a religious fair. The word means a place where people meet. There are about forty melas held in Benares every year, and they are attended by thousands of people.

We visited one of these religious festivals a little while ago. It was held in a small village, a few miles away from Benares. The people came together to celebrate the birth of their great god Rām. Thousands of people were gathered round the lake just outside the village. All sorts of things were on sale—dolls, hats, necklaces, and books. There were plenty of sweets of every description, and for these there was a great demand. Then there were swings and merry-go-rounds, which the people appeared to enjoy immensely. At one of these fairs I saw a holy man buried in the ground right up to his neck, and

INDIAN CHRISTIAN WORKERS AT MELA.
Photo by C. P. Cape]

PRESSING THE SUGAR CANE—A VILLAGE SCENE.
[*Photo by C. P. Cape*

close by was one of Edison's phonographs, to the long tubes of which a number of rustics had attached themselves!

There were several men present with gambling-tables. These did a very brisk business in the main street of the village, until, at our instigation, the constables appeared and confiscated all the apparatus.

The police are always present in force at these fairs. And they are often needed, for in the crush and rush of the multitude the thief has his opportunity. He brutally snatches a nose-ring from some poor woman and disappears in the crowd. The woman, her face bathed with blood, appeals to the police, who take her before the magistrate to make her statement. The constables apprehend all suspicious-looking individuals, and the inspector orders them behind the tent to have their backs examined. If old scars proclaim them to be old criminals, they will be sent to the lock-up on suspicion, while further inquiries are made. Many women and girls are brutally murdered in India for the sake of their jewellery.

To break the rush of the crowds in some of the temples, several burly policemen are stationed with long, strong knotted towels, round about the shrine. As the people rush madly on to make their offerings to the god, the police endeavour to keep order by striking the worshippers with their long wet cloths!

The rice and the pice go to the priests, and the gods get the smell. And everybody seems content.

In some spots the Christian must walk carefully, on account of the muster of people who are getting a shave and a hair-cut. The shave is done without soap, and spares nothing except the sacred lock. The hair is supposed to be ethically unclean, the abode of evil spirits and the seat of bad magnetism. So it must be sacrificed. The women retain their hair. Of course, if they are widows, their heads must always be kept shaven.

At some of these melas, the people stay for two or three days, resting at night under a pipal or nīm tree. Then the missionary with a magic-lantern has an opening. When the day dawns, he will go on with his preaching and distribution of Christian literature.

It is pretty certain that the booths and the shows and the shops and the social intercourse help to make these religious festivals popular. They certainly give the missionary a splendid opportunity for preaching the gospel.

With so few workers, how can the glad tidings be sent to the 102,000 villages of the United Provinces?

In the big melas the people come to us. And then they hear of Christ, most of them for the first and the last time.

CHAPTER XXVI.

AN OUTPOST.

ONE day, several winters ago, we entered a town with a population of about two thousand souls. The place had been visïted by missionaries some years before, but there was no Christian school or worker in the little town. So we decided to open a mission school. It was very difficult to rent a house, because most of the people were Muhammadans and bitterly opposed to us. At last a retired inspector of police was persuaded to rent us a large, dirty room for which we were to pay five shillings a month. The boys came slowly. Their parents were suspicious. Lying reports were spread abroad. Then the plague came. Some of our boys died. Then the landlord told us we must give up his room. His neighbours had decided that if he continued to let us have the use of

AN INDIAN BARBER.
Photo by C. P. Cape]

THE ELEPHANT'S BATH.
[*Photo by C. P. Cape*

it, he would be excommunicated. That is to say, he would not be allowed to smoke with them, nor would he be able to marry his children according to their position. He gave us notice to quit. We decided to get some land and build. A wealthy, generous Indian prince offered to give us some land, and sent his agent to arrange matters. The first plot was suitable, but we could not accept it as it was next to the Muhammadans' slaughter-house, and no Hindu would have sent his boy to a school so situated. Then a piece of land between two small lakes was offered, and we were about to accept it with many thanks, when an old farmer was heard to mutter something. 'What is he saying?' I asked the preacher, for it is generally very difficult to understand the villagers. 'Oh,' was the reply, 'he says that in the rainy season those two lakes overflow, and that piece of land disappears beneath the water!' So, as we could not afford to build a light-house with a school in the top room, we had to decline the offer.

One day we visited an Indian gentleman

and told him of our need. He at once promised to help, and not long after he gave us a plot of land just outside the town and near the railway-station. Before we could build, it was necessary to remove a tree which stood in the middle of the ground. But the tree belonged to some other man, and he was not willing to part with it. We had got the land, but not the tree which grew on it! When Abraham bought the field of Ephron, 'the field, and the cave which was therein, and all the trees that were in the field . . . were made sure unto Abraham.' We had got the field without the tree! But at last we persuaded the owner to sell, and then we began to build. Four times one of the walls fell down. We sent for the builder and asked for an explanation. 'While digging the foundations,' he informed us, 'we came across a skull and some bones; the spirits of the dead object to our intrusion, and being angry with us, cause the walls to fall.' That was his excuse; but when you know that this man and his men were being paid by the day for their work, you may be able to discover another explanation.

At last the school and teacher's house were finished; we built them both for forty pounds.

We cannot persuade many boys to attend, because they can earn good money by carpet-weaving, for this town is in the centre of the famous Mirzapur carpet industry. But the school gives the teacher a good standing, and in the evenings he is able to preach the gospel in the bazaars and the villages round about. And it is encouraging to reflect that every day some thirty Moslem and Hindu boys are being taught Christian truths, through Christian hymns and the Christian's Bible.

CHAPTER XXVII.

OPENING AN OUT-STATION.

If people in England think that all the people of India are calling out for missionaries they make a great mistake. As a rule, the people are quite willing to do without us. So we were agreeably surprised when one of our preachers told us that the chief landowners at K—— wanted us to open a school in their village. There was no doubt about it, the men were in earnest; they actually sent a conveyance. Can you guess what it was? It was not a horse, or a cart, or a bicycle, or a motor-car. It was an elephant! It came about five in the morning. How were we to mount? The driver explained: 'You stand on his leg and then put your foot in the twist I make in his tail, and then some one gives you a push from behind—and there you are'! Well sometimes

VILLAGE DONKEYS.

[*Photo by C. P. Cape*

HEAVY-LADEN VILLAGERS.

[*Photo by C. P. Cape*

there you are, and sometimes there you aren't!

Then we started off. I sat on the elephant's neck, my wife sat on his back, and the evangelist sat on what was left. It was a small elephant, and it looked quite crowded.

As we got into the jungle, we saw several jackals hurrying home, and many village people carrying wood and dung and earthen pots to sell in Benares.

The small children in the villages were very excited when they saw us. They ran after the elephant and put their hands and faces in its foot-prints! Some of the bigger boys and girls managed to touch its tail. You see it reminds them of their great god Ganesha, the one who brings good luck to his worshippers. This god has an elephant's head and a very big stomach.

The Muhammadan mahout (all the elephant-drivers here are Muhammadans), when I asked him if he also worshipped his charge, smiled and said: 'God is but one, the Unseen.' But one must not think that all these Moslems are good because their creed seems good. They don't know that God is a God of Holy Love.

Once we got to some steep, broken ground, and Moti (the elephant) had to climb. The driver gave warning, but a little too late, and in a moment our catechist had slipped off over the animal's tail. 'A good thing it was a baby elephant,' he said, as he clambered up again.

It was now ten o'clock, and as the sun was well up, and we were getting hot and tired, a rest was suggested. In a few minutes we had about twenty people round us. We sang a hymn, and the catechist spoke to them, and after having prayed for them, we went on our way.

About mid-day the elephant got thirsty and tired, and suddenly made a bolt for a big pond. When he had taken in sufficient water to make the fishes anxious, he began to bathe. This he could do with the greatest of ease, because every elephant has in his trunk a most efficient shower-bath. Fortunately for us on his back, he was persuaded by the mahout to confine his activities to the lower regions.

At last the village was reached, and we were glad. Elephant riding is very nice if taken in small quantities.

We were conducted by our preacher to a temple court-yard, where all the important land-owners were waiting for us. We moved on to the traveller's rest-house, and then the farmers made their request. There was no school in the village and none in the neighbourhood, and they would be glad if we would open one. They would give us a room for the school, they would give our teacher a house, they would pay good fees, and they would not object to religious instruction.

Three weeks after, a teacher was sent to open a school. 'You shall not enter our village,' the people cried. 'You have got the plague and want to give it to us; you have brought fowls with you and you will kill and eat them; you must not come here: go away.' But late at night they somewhat relented, and let the poor fellow and his wife go into an empty house.

Now when we heard what had happened,

we went over to see what could be done. Things had quieted down, and the headman told us he was very sorry the ignorant people had treated our teacher with so little respect. 'I am but one,' said he, 'and what can I do?'

As we were walking round the village, some men came up to me and said, 'Please do not give us the plague; please do not look at our children; do not go so near to our wells.'

With many words we tried to allay their fears, but they seemed glad when we turned away.

In this small village there is a big temple, and we heard that some of the priests did not want us to enter the place. But things have now greatly changed. Our teacher is the best-known and most respected man in the village. He and his wife have won the hearts of the people by their unfailing tact and sympathy.

One winter we pitched our tent just outside this village. We had some medicines with us, but nothing very dangerous—quinine and permanganate of potash! The first patient was an old farmer. 'Twenty-five years ago, O Protector of the Poor, a splinter entered my left eye and damaged the sight; will your honour be so good as to apply a remedy?'

So I looked at the quinine and at the permanganate of potash, and finally decided that my friend had better go to the hospital, which was only ten miles away.

Most of the patients were ill with fever, and we were often able to help by giving them quinine. The village post-offices sell this drug in farthing packets, and all our catechists keep a supply of this wonderful medicine, which is much needed in a country where, in one year, over four millions die of fever.

Our little school in this village is doing very well. The people now do not urge us to go away; but they often ask the teacher, 'When is the missionary coming to see us again?'

CHAPTER XXVIII.

IN THE VILLAGES.

We pitched our tent at K——, about eighteen miles north-west of Benares. The village is quite small, but famous for its temple. In the bazaar, sweets and marigolds are the chief commodities. The latter are grown in large quantities, and are used for garlands in the temple. In the lake close by, the people do their washing, and perform their ablutions and worship. The elephants are bathed in the water. And the people drink it without getting enteric. The dogs of the village are many, large, starved, scared, and demonstrative. The people are ignorant and superstitious, and many of them take intoxicants.

Some time ago, at the request of several of the leading landowners, we opened a school in this village, and there are now about thirty boys attending. A Hindu teaches them Hindi and arithmetic; and our evangelist does his best to impart Christian knowledge, without unduly shocking the religious prejudice of parents and priests. Not that our designs are hidden, for the Creed and the Ten Commandments are conspicuously displayed on the school verandah, while dazzling pictures of Daniel in the lion's den, and of the Brazen Serpent, declare our intentions to the inquiring passer-by. Sixteen shillings is paid yearly for the rent of the house in which our evangelist lives, and in the front of which the boys sit and vociferously recite their lessons.

A night or two after our arrival, a magic-lantern entertainment was given outside the tent. It can hardly be called a lantern service, as some of the slides had a secular tendency. When the well-known moving picture of the rat-swallowing sleeper appeared on the sheet, the evangelist, thinking it must have a moral, explained to the wondering audience that this was the fruit of drunkenness.

But on another night, when this same slide was shown for the amusement of the children, one of our younger preachers informed the listeners that the swallower of rats was a victim of the opium habit! All the slides were not of this nature, for we followed with 'Probable Sons,' 'The Pilgrim's Progress,' and finished with some scenes in the life of our Lord, which seemed to impress the people deeply. We thought we had been generous enough in allowing all to come without charge or collection, and were not a little surprised by a man asking next day how much we would give him if he attended the entertainment!

In the mornings we visited the neighbouring villages, but were not welcomed in many. The people thought we were employed by the government to relieve the pressure of population by spreading the plague. 'The very next day after the missionary visited our village, a rat dead of plague was found in my house,' a farmer gravely informed his friends.

In one place the people allowed us to

sing a hymn, and then, with unwelcome generosity, urged us to preach the gospel in the regions beyond. 'We will get our young men to beat you if you don't go quickly,' shrieked some excited women. A sturdy oil-seller emphasized their wishes by an attempt to remove me forcibly from my seat. As the men were armed with sickles and pruning-hooks, and we had only our books and tracts, we judged it expedient to meet their wishes, and so turned homeward.

Passing through another village, an old man bowed himself down to the ground, and, addressing me, said: 'You are our prince, you are our god, by your clemency we are nourished, you are as God.' Upon hearing which, our Indian minister said to me: 'You are like Paul; defied in one place, deified in another.'

One Friday afternoon we went to a village and preached in the bazaar to about sixty people. One man was undisguisedly hostile. 'What is the meaning of Masih (Christ)?' he asked. 'Anointed, sent by God," was the reply. 'Oh!' said he, 'in our village it means buffalo.' Our youngest preacher raised his stick to avenge the insult to his religion. 'Don't do that; put your stick down, and I will call the bazaar superintendent,' the missionary cried. 'Go, and I will wait for thee,' the man shrieked. But by the time the superintendent had arrived, the bold interrupter had decided to retreat. Such incidents are extremely rare, as the people generally listen quietly and with respect to our message.

One evening the magic-lantern was taken to this village. After a tedious search, a blank wall in a suitable position was found, and on this we fastened our sheet. But there was no stand for the lantern. 'You can use my camel's back, missionary,' said one of the interested onlookers. The offer was politely refused, and on three dirty old rickety oil-boxes, which had to be most judiciously balanced, the lantern was placed, and the proceedings opened with the rat-swallowing sleeper.

We have now a school of thirty boys in this village, who are taught Hindi, arithmetic, Christian hymns, and the catechism.

One day, while resting in a small shed near the bazaar, we saw some farmers buying some cloth from two Panjabi merchants. Although the purchases did not exceed a rupee (1s. 4*d.*), the money was not paid down. The merchant entered in his book the sum due, the buyer's name, his father's name, his caste and his village; and he hoped to collect the accounts when the spring crops are harvested next year.

One day we were asked to see the village goldsmith, who was very ill. The room was about eight feet long, eight feet broad, and six feet high. It had one window, which was closed. It had one door, which was shut. About twenty people were crowded into the room. The man was clearly dying. 'What has been your treatment?' I asked the doctor. 'I have caused him to fast for some days,' was the reply. For ten days no food nor stimulant nor medicine had entered his lips. Next day, death delivered him from the doctor.

S——, a village of 1,200 people, we

visited by train. We called on the inspector of police, and found him a civil and intelligent Muhammadan. He informed us that many of the criminal class lived in his district. 'I caught one coiner,' said he; 'the man offered me a hundred rupees to release him, which I refused; but he will get off; he will give ten rupees to this man, and twenty rupees to that man, and he will probably escape conviction. I do not take bribes,' he continued, 'but many people do.' He had never heard of a missionary visiting that village before.

A day or two before our tent was removed, we paid a final visit to S——. A friendly landowner lent us his elephant.

As we entered the bazaar, the vegetables and grain displayed in abundance on every side attracted the interest of Moti Lāl, the elephant; and in spite of the efforts of the mahout and the shop-keepers, he proceeded to sample the produce.

Forgetting or ignoring the respect due to the beast, the angry merchants struck him on the head and trunk with their long sticks. But others, perhaps those who had not been robbed, offered ample compensation for the insults, by bowing before him as he passed and by touching reverently his tail and footprints. 'Defied in one place and deified in another,' is perhaps again a legitimate comment.

A friend suggests that I should explain how we preach in the villages. Well, here is a typical case.

Having pacified the dogs, we looked for the cleanest bed, under the shadiest tree. We sat down on as little of that bed as possible. Then we sang in Hindi :

> The world, my brother! will abide with none,
> By the world's Maker let thy heart be won.

A few people gathered, and when we had finished the hymn, one of the evangelists spoke, taking the hymn as his text. When he had done, another preacher did his best to show how much strength in life and death the Christian believer finds, in comparison with his Hindu brother.

Many questions were asked ; especially as to what comes after death. The goldsmith, who had been listening attentively, affirmed the doctrine of transmigration, and we tried to show him a more excellent way. Then we prayed for the people, that they and theirs might be saved from snakes and robbers, and might come to know the God and Father of Jesus Christ. 'We pray like this for you every day,' we told them, at which they all seemed quite pleased. We said farewell and left them, giving a tract in Hindi or Urdu to any who could read. And this is the way we have preached the gospel in the villages.

Time and money have been expended in this work; what are the gains? Some of the people are now quite sure that we are not employed by the government to spread the plague. Several of the leading landowners are inclined to be friendly; and since we returned from camp, have paid us formal visits. The catechists working in the villages have been instructed and encouraged. Hundreds of people have heard of Jesus Christ. Some of them have now the Word of God in their possession.

As for ourselves, we have more fully realized the vastness of our work, the need of impressing our friends at home with some sense of its magnitude, and the necessity for a greater reliance on the co-operating and confirming ministry of the Holy Spirit.

CHAPTER XXIX.

OPEN-AIR PREACHING.

We preach regularly in the bazaars of Benares. The superintendent, an Indian minister, a catechist and two or three students, complete our staff. We take our stand by the side of one of the main roads and not far from a mosque. The harmonium or concertina sounds, and the meeting begins with a Christian hymn sung to some native tune. Slowly the crowd gathers. If Muhammadans predominate, a Persian 'ghazal' is sung; if Hindus, an Indian 'bhajan.'

A band of pilgrims passes, carrying large jars of Ganges water for the benefit of themselves and their friends in some distant village home. They are all agriculturalists. They are all caste Hindus. When these are won for Christ, the end will be near. When all the out-castes of

BAZAAR PREACHING, BENARES. [Photo by Saeed Bros., Benares

India are gathered in—and may that time come speedily !—the Christian Church will still be faced by a task of unparalleled importance, the conversion of the Moslems and the caste Hindus of the great peninsula.

The pilgrims stop for a few minutes. It is difficult to keep their attention long. They have been to the holy city and bathed in the sacred stream. They are saved. What interest, then, can they have in our message, which is for the lost ?

They pass on, and probably will never hear of Christ again. From the mosque close by come several Moslems, who listen with close attention. They have the greatest respect for Hazrat Isa, the Christian's prophet. They delight to hear idolatry denounced. But when sins of the flesh are denounced, some of them smile and others move away.

The preacher speaks of the great revelation of God through His Son Jesus Christ. 'Blasphemy, blasphemy !' they cry. And they too have gone.

Here is an intelligent-looking young

man. 'I am Aryā Samāj,' he says, speaking in English; 'please tell me, sir, if you really think that the whale swallowed Jonah?' He is told that he must wait till the preaching is over, and then his question will be answered.

One day one of our catechists was telling the old, old story of the prodigal son. To avoid offending the susceptibilities of his Hindu listeners, he departed from the text of Scripture, and cried, 'The father said, Let us kill the fatted goat.' 'No, not goat, calf,' corrected a small Hindu boy who attended a mission school. But the preacher, still thinking more of consistency than veracity, exclaimed, 'So they killed the fatted goat.' The small boy turned away repeating, 'It wasn't a goat, it was a calf.'

Here comes a temple-priest. He listens, with a haughty smile on his proud face. 'You speak of sin,' he cries; 'what is sin?' Disloyalty to God, he is told. 'What is God?' he asks. And then you find how far your thoughts are from his. That is the open-air preacher's difficulty in India.

God, Sin, Salvation, Holiness, you can translate these words into the language of your listeners, that is an easy thing to do. But those four words do not mean to the Hindu and the Moslem what they mean to you. 'Christ can give you salvation,' is your message. And the passing stranger understands you to say that Christ can save you from being born again, He can cause you to be quickly re-absorbed into the Great Source of all things!

One day, preaching in a bazaar, an old Muhammadan interrupted. The missionary had been speaking on Paul's declaration, 'I am not ashamed of the gospel; for it is the power of God unto salvation to every one that believeth.' The old man cried aloud before the people, 'Sir, where is the power to be seen? I have lived in a military town, and I know that your Christian soldiers go to the bazaars at night to commit sin. Where, then, is the power of Christianity?'

The Moslem was told that all Europeans are not Christians, and that the gospel 'is the power of God unto salvation, *to every one that believeth.'* But the missionary will not soon forget that interruption.

As a rule, Christian literature is offered for sale at our open-air meetings.

Many years ago, a little lad visited Benares on pilgrimage with his father. They heard some Christian missionaries preaching. They bought a Gospel. That was the beginning. The end is not yet. But that little lad is to-day one of our ordained missionaries in South India.

BENARES DOMS.

CHAPTER XXX.

BENARES DOMS.

THESE people are probably of Dravidian origin. There are about twelve hundred of them in the Benares district. Some of them are engaged as burners of the dead, and others are employed as scavengers. On account of their occupation, they are despised and hated by all Hindus.

Not a few of the men are thieves, and some of the women worse. They have drink, sloth, and lust in their very bones and blood. They have been given a bad name, and they have certainly tried hard to deserve it.

Amongst the gipsy Doms, a bride costs six shillings and eightpence, ten pounds of treacle, a sheet, five lumps of tobacco, and five packets of betel leaf. The women must be tattooed. They all have a superstitious reverence for iron, and a mother will keep a knife on her bed, beside her newly-born baby, to ward off evil spirits.

Not a few of the women are employed in making baskets, fans, &c., so that in this respect as well as in name, they have something in common with the European gipsies (Romany). And, as has been said, they are not all honest.

The sister's husband officiates as priest when they worship Gandak or Bhawāni. To the latter a young pig is sometimes offered in sacrifice, its flesh being eaten by the worshipper.

The reason of their coming to Benares is an interesting one. The story was told by a European superintendent of police. Many years ago, it appears, there was a Muhammadan inspector of police who was not content with his official salary. The perquisites of his position were not as substantial as he desired. So he sent a request to an officer of police at Calcutta that he would dispatch to Benares a few Dom families. In due time they arrived, and were ordered to appear at the police-station. And it was duly arranged that they should pursue their usual avocation, and should share their booty with the inspector!

Let it not be thought, however, that all the Doms are thieves. Quite a number of them at the present time are employed by the Municipality as street-sweepers, and receive for their work a monthly wage of five shillings and fourpence. A fair proportion even of these have at some time or another been in prison. Not that this fact is necessarily much to their discredit. For if a robbery has been committed, and the actual perpetrator cannot be traced, it is quite likely that suspicion will fall on the nearest Doms, and if they cannot furnish security for good behaviour, they will be sent to prison for twelve months. The sections of the Penal Code which make this possible are liable to abuse when used and enforced by some Indian police and magistrates. There are probably hundreds of people in Indian prisons because they are too poor to provide the required security.

Our work amongst these vagabonds

began about two years ago. Their gipsy life makes it difficult for us to give them the instruction they need. The demons of lust and drink fight hard for the Dom. 'Our first and principal aim is to get him under the influence of a better man than himself.'

When these people came to us for baptism, their motives were not unmixed. They desire to flee from the wrath that now is, from hunger and oppression, as well as, probably more than, from the wrath to come. They think the missionary can help them, that he has 'bread enough and to spare.'

But there is every reason to hope that they will have higher motives and deeper longings when they know more of the Bread of Life.

We are trying to instruct their children. But sometimes it seems that the influences of home counteract any good that may have been imparted in the mission school. And as even small boys and girls can earn a few shillings a month by street-sweeping, it is impossible to persuade the parents to make the sacrifice necessarily involved in sending them to school. Two little lads whose parents are in prison are being trained in one of our orphanages.

Our first convert is perhaps the best. He is now the chapel-keeper. His changed life is a splendid witness to his new religion. He is the proud possessor of a medal which he received for taking part in the Tibet campaign. He was not a soldier, he did not fight. He was only a scavenger. And he was a Dom, a man whose touch would hopelessly defile even a corpse. But as he had shared in the dangers and privations of the expedition, the British government awarded him the medal, bearing the image and superscription of the King-Emperor.

There are only twelve hundred of these people in the Benares district. But there are nearly 60,000,000 out-castes in India; and at present the Christian Church is winning her triumphs mainly amongst these. Nor is any apology offered, or necessary, for this fact. They are God's property. By caring for the out-caste, the Church reveals to all her Lord's estimate of humanity.

We may not reach the Hindu's intellect with our philosophy, but surely this loving service rendered to the lowly will touch his heart. Christ is best preached by exhibiting His Spirit in Christ-like deeds.

CHAPTER XXXI.

TULSI DĀS.

In Benares is a landing-stage called the Tulsi Dās ghāt, because the famous Hindu poet lived close by.

He was born in 1532, probably at Tarī in the Doāb. Deserted by his parents, he was adopted by a sādhu, who probably gave him his name, according to a custom which these men have. When they desire to purify any person, they cause him to eat a tulasi leaf which has been dedicated to an image of Vishnu.

He was much influenced by his wife, who called him to devote his love to Rāma rather than to any earthly object. Tulsi Dās then became a wandering ascetic. After some years he settled in Ayodhya, and there began to write his famous poems. Having some differences with the Vairāgi Vaishnava about eating and drinking, he removed to Benares and lived for years at Asi-ghāt, near Lotarka-Kund.

It is said that one day, after he had finished his great poem, he was bathing at Maṇikarnika ghāt, when a pandit, who was proud of his knowledge of Sanskrit, came up to him and said, 'Reverend sir, your honour is a learned Sanskrit pandit; why therefore did your Honour compose an epic poem in the vulgar tongue?' Tulsi Dās replied, 'My language in the vulgar tongue is imperfect, I admit, but it is better than the erotics of your Sanskrit-knowing gentlemen.' 'How is that?' said the pandit. 'Because,' said Tulsi Dās, 'If thou find a jewelled vessel full of poison and an earthen cup full of ambrosia, which wilt thou refuse and which wilt thou accept?'

It is to the glory of God and the eternal honour of Tulsi Dās, that from the beginning to the end of his Rāmāyan, there is not one impure thought to be found. And this is more than can be said of Valmīki's Rāmāyan, which nevertheless is the source and inspiration of the great Hindi epic.

Tulsi Dās taught a belief in a personal Supreme Being, and that, to redeem man God became incarnate, and that He is waiting to be gracious still to all who call upon Him.

Tulsi Dās's poem is a 'passionate protest against the virtual atheism of philosophical Hindu theology,' which, as Dr. Thibaut says, 'is too little in sympathy with the wants of the human heart, which, after all, are not so very different in India from what they are elsewhere. Comparatively few, even in India, are those who rejoice in the idea of a universal non-personal essence, in which their own individuality is to be merged and lost for ever, who think it is sweet 'to be wrecked on the ocean of the Infinite.' The only religious books of wide-spread influence are such as the Rāmāyan of Tulsi Dās which . . . love to dwell on the delights of devotion to the one all-wise and merciful ruler who is able and willing to lend a gracious ear to the supplication of the worshipper.'

The famous poem of Tulsi Dās was

begun in March, 1574. Fortunately for India, Rāma and not Krishna is the divine-human hero of the epic. The poem is divided into seven sections, Childhood, Ayodhya, The Forest, Kishkindhya, The Beautiful, Lanka, and the Sequel.

In 'The Forest' chapter, we are told how Rāwan, the demon-king of Ceylon, abducted Sīta, Rām's beloved wife, while her husband was in pursuit of Mārīcha, who had taken the form of a spotted deer. A friendly vulture comes to her assistance, but is mortally wounded by Rāwan. Rāma finds him and cries—I use Mr. Growse's translation—" Remain alive, father." He smiled and answered: " He, by the repetition of whose name at the hour of death the vilest sinner . . attains salvation, has come in bodily form before my eyes; what need is there, sire, for me to live any longer?" Rāma's eyes filled with tears as he replied: " It is your own good deeds that have saved you. There is nothing in the world beyond the reach of those who devote their soul to the good of others." '

Then a woman meets Rāma and cries, 'How can I hymn thy praises, seeing that I am of meanest descent and dullest wit; the lowest of the low and a woman to boot—O sinless god?' Said Rāma in reply: 'Hearken, lady, to my words: I recognize no kinsmanship save that of faith; neither lineage, family, religion, rank, wealth, power, connexions, virtue, nor ability. A man without faith is of no more account than a cloud without water.'

In the section, 'Beautiful,' Sīta is repelling Rāwan's advances. 'I tell you, you are but a glow-worm, while the very sun is only an image of Rāma.' Hearing this, Rāwan threatens to kill the lady, who replies: 'My lord's arms, Rāwan, are beautiful as a string of dark lotuses, and mighty as an elephant's trunk; either they shall have my neck, or if not, then your cruel sword.'

Hanumān, the monkey-king, now appears to Sita and brings her a ring which Rāma has given as a token.

Rāma, with a great army of bears and

monkeys, advances to rescue Sīta. Rāwan's wife advises her husband not to fight against Rāma, but at once to relinquish Sīta. But his ministers remind him how he has conquered gods and demons, and counsel him to fight. Then says the poet: 'When these three, a minister, a physician, and a spiritual adviser, use fair words, either from fear or hope of reward, dominion, religion, and health are all three quickly destroyed.'

Rāwan's brother, Vibhīshan, gives the demon-king good advice: 'Lust, passion, vanity, and covetousness are all paths that lead to hell: abjure them and worship Rāma, whom all the saints worship. Rāma, my brother, is no mortal king, but the sovereign of the universe, the Fate of Fate itself, the Supreme Spirit, the imperishable and uncreated god, the benefactor of cows and of Brahmans, of the earth and of the gods; who in his infinite mercy has assumed the form of humanity, to rejoice his votaries and to break the ranks of the impious.' But Rāwan replies: 'You live in my capital, but are in love with hermits; you had better go to them, if you want to preach.'

Vibhīshan decides to go over to Rāma. Some are suspicious of him; but Rāma replies: 'I would not abandon any one who had fled to me for protection, even though he had been guilty of the murder of a million Brahmans. Directly any creature appears before me, I blot out the sins of all his past lives. No one who is essentially wicked can delight in my service; if he is really bad at heart, how can he come into my presence? Only a man of pure soul can find me.'

Rāwan's wife again tries to dissuade her husband from the encounter. 'But,' says the poet, 'though the clouds rain ambrosia upon it, the bamboo neither flowers nor fruits; so the soul of a fool never learns, though he have Brahmans and Shiva for his teachers.'

Hanumān appears before Rāwan, and amongst other things, says to him: 'There is no valour shown in slaying the slain. Now an outcast, a man mad with lust, a miser, a destitute beggar, a man in disgrace, a man in extreme old age, one who is always ill or always in a passion, a rebel against Vishnu, a hater of religion and the saints, a man who thinks only of his own body, a scandal-monger and a man thoroughly vicious, these twelve, while they live are no better than corpses. On this account, wretch, I do not slay you.'

Rāwan's conceit is compared to the sandpiper's, which goes to sleep with its legs in the air and thinks that they help to support the sky!

The fight begins. 'Taking each a demon in his clutch, the monkeys ran off and dropt to the ground with the enemy beneath and themselves on top.'

A warrior, as huge as a mountain, approaches. 'Millions upon millions of mountain peaks did the bears and monkeys cast upon him.'

At the end, Rāwan is killed, and his wife laments, 'Jackals devour your hands and arms; and rightly so, seeing that you opposed Rāma . . . you heeded not my words and took the sovereign of all things . . . for a mere man . . . you took for a man, the self-existent, . . . and you worshipped not the all-merciful, . . . and yet Rāma has now raised you to his own abode. I bow before the blameless god.'

Before the final encounter with Rāwan, Vibhīshan notices that Rāma has no chariot, and becoming anxious, inquires how he can hope to conquer so powerful a warrior. 'Hearken, friend,' replied the all-merciful, 'a conqueror has a different kind of chariot. Manliness and courage are his chariot wheels; unflinching truthfulness and morality his banners and standards; strength, discretion, self-control and benevolence his horses, with grace, mercy and equanimity for their harness; prayer to Mahādeva his unerring charioteer; continence his shield, contentment his sword, alms-giving his axe, knowledge his mighty spear, and perfect science his stout bow. His pure and constant soul stands for a quiver, his pious practices of devotion for a sheath of arrows, and the revenue he pays to Brahmans, and his guru is his imperishable coat of mail. There is no equipment for victory that can be compared to this, nor is there any enemy, my friend, who can conquer the man who takes his stand on the chariot of religion.'

Sīta is recovered. She successfully endures 'the fire, which tests all men's actions'; it becomes as cool as sandalwood on her entering it, and she is restored to Rāma.

The sixth book closes with these words: 'The wise, who listen to the achievements of Rāma and his victory in the battle, God rewards for ever with victory, wisdom, and renown. This sinful age is the very home of impurity: think well on it, and understand that if you abandon the blessed name of Rāma, there is no other saviour.'

In the last book we read of 'the happiness and prosperity of the city of Avadh, when Rāma reigned as king.' Says Tulsi Dās, in conclusion, 'Without affection there is no finding Rāma, though you have recourse to meditation, prayer, sacrifice, and asceticism.'

'O my brother, there is no religion like charity, and no meanness like malevolence.'

Dr. G. A. Grierson, I.C.S., to whom we

are indebted for most of what we know about Tulsi Dās, tells us that the dying words of the great poet were: 'I have sung the glory of the name of Rāma, and now would I be silent. Now place ye the gold and the leaf of tulasi into Tulsi's mouth.'

Tulsi Dās was a contemporary of our Shakespeare, and was alive when the Authorized Version was being translated. But so far as we can discover, he never came under the influence of Christianity. Seeing that his great poem, the Rāmāyan, is known and loved by many millions of the people of North India, we may rejoice at the measure of truth it contains, and we may be sure that men who can appreciate the purity, the meekness, the self-sacrifice of Rāma, will worship the Lord Jesus Christ, when they know Him.

CHAPTER XXXII.

SOME SUPERSTITIONS.

I FOUND most of these in an old book, but as my pandit has given his word that the people of these parts believe in them to-day, you can accept them as correct. When a man yawns, he fillips two of the fingers of his left hand. My book says that no one can tell the reason of this; but the pandit informs me that by fillipping the fingers, evil spirits, which live in the air, and might enter the open mouth with dire results, are frightened far away.

It is considered unlucky to sell anything on credit the first thing in the morning. The shop-keeper will often sell an article at a slightly reduced price in order that he may get cash for his first sale and so ensure a good day's business.

No one should mention a child's name at night. If an owl should happen to hear,

THE MUHARRAM PROCESSION IN BENARES.

[*Photo by Saeed Bros., Benares*

the bird might repeat the name ; and with the repetition, the child would pine away and die.

If our watchman hears an owl hooting at night, close by our house, he tries to frighten it away. He tells us that the owl's hoot means that some one will die.

If a child is allowed to use a looking-glass before it has teethed, the process of teething will be very painful for it.

The word 'bujhānā' means to extinguish. But no wife may say 'bujhāo' the lamp, because the husband is the light of the house and she would be praying for his death. So she says, 'make the lamp cold.'

The word for snake, 'sānp,' must never be used at night, for the reptile would probably come in the darkness if he heard his name. So a snake at night must be called 'Kīrā,' that is, a worm, or 'Rassī,' that is, a rope.

The mothers believe that the evil spirits are glad to get hold of their children to make them ill or to kill them. So each mother tries to persuade the 'bhūts,' as they are called, that her child is not worthy of their attention. With this end in view she tells her neighbours how weak and sickly the baby is, when perhaps, as a matter of fact, it is quite healthy and strong! Sometimes a parent will call her child 'Fly,' or 'Grasshopper,' or even 'Dung-heap,' so that the spirits may think it too mean for their diversion.

I knew a woman who had lost several children. When a new baby came, she put it in a very dirty basket and sold it—for five minutes—to a neighbour for some small shells worth about the twentieth part of a farthing! She did this to deceive the demons. A boy is sometimes clothed and adorned as a girl, with a similar end in view.

Although the Hindu regards the monkey as a very sacred animal, he thinks it most unlucky to see one early in the morning.

It is considered most unpropitious to hear any one sneeze when you are about to begin some work, or to start on a journey.

Here is a list of evil omens:—To see a

blind man; to hear any one cry as you leave the house; to hear a crow caw on a decayed tree; to see a snake cross one's path; to meet a widow or a cat; to be overtaken by men carrying a dead body; to see an empty pitcher.

And here is a list of some good omens:—To see a dead man being carried along without any mourner; to see a fox cross your path from left to right; to see a Brahman with uncovered head; to see a crow sitting on a dead body floating down the river; to hear the sound of a sacred shell in a temple; to see a pitcher with a rope tied to it; to meet with a dancing-woman.

I asked my pandit why it was good-luck to meet with a dancing-woman, and this was his answer: 'You see, sir, that our dancing-girls never marry, and a woman who never marries can never be a widow.'

CHAPTER XXXIII.

SOME INDIAN SAYINGS.

If God orders you to pull, He will give you a rope; if He wants you to ride, He will give you a horse.

If your heart be pure, the Ganges is in your tub.

Eggs and oaths are soon broken.

To-day's egg is better than to-morrow's hen.

Man is man's enemy.

Man is man's remedy.

No man will build himself a hut, until he has got wet; no man will stoop until he has bumped his head.

If you lend, you may lose money and friend.

He has a head,—and so has a pin!

He who does not climb, will not fall.

To swallow the camel and choke at the tail.

AN INDIAN ASCETIC. (His left arm is useless).

By a native artist]

AN INDIAN ASCETIC.

[*By a native artist*

One and one make eleven (11).

Kill one, a murderer: kill thousands, a hero.

The little pot soon boils.

A little praise is a curse.

Contentment is great wealth.

Straighten a dog's tail for twelve years, it will still curl.

Shut a crow in a cage, will it talk like a parrot?

The jackal's howl hurts not my buffalo, nor does the abuse of the angry hurt me.

Does the dog's barking or the cock's crowing make the day break?

The bow always bent becomes slack.

Beauty without purity is an odourless rose.

The wound will heal; but the scar will show.

Flint is cold, but it contains fire.

When dead, then you will be straight.

Who lives in the river should court the crocodile.

Why trouble to count the miles of a road you need not travel?

Lift carefully the cloth which has fallen on the thorns.

Don't throw away the rudder because you are near the shore.

Three men can keep a secret—when two of them are dead.

The world's praise is a puff of wind.

Prayer is the pillar of piety.

He who pursues two hares will catch neither.

Strike the lute before the buffalo; it will stand and chew the cud.

By caring for cowries, wealth is won.

Hunger is the best chutney.

To invite Satan is easy, to dismiss him is hard.

We give to God the flower beyond our reach.

Prepare for death, but sow your field.

Light your lamp at home, afterwards at the mosque.

It takes time to be successful, but no time to be ruined.

Musk is known by the smell, not by the praise of the perfumer.

If you've never seen a 'thug,' look at a publican!

Do your work and let the curs bark.

Under a tree, there lived a ho
Day by day he clasped his ha
closed his eyes and cried aloud : '
draw me to thyself to day ! ' No
lived in the village close by, a wa
day he bought a rope, and went
with it till he came behind the tre
the saint prayed. He climbed i
tree without attracting notice.
prepared a loose-knot in the r
waited. Presently the prayer ag
offered. ' O Lord, draw me to thy
day ! ' Upon hearing these wo
wag let down the rope over the
head, and began to haul.

As soon as he felt himself rising
air, and realized that his prayer wa
to be answered, he cried out in his
' Not to-day, O Lord, not to-da
morrow ! '

CHAPTER XXXIV.

THE WAY OF SALVATION.

THE desire of the serious Hindu is to obtain as much merit as possible. He believes that all his bad deeds will be reckoned against him, so he performs certain meritorious acts which will be counted to his credit, and which will, he hopes, counterbalance his evil deeds.

If the issue is in his favour when he dies, he expects to find his position improved when he is born again.

That some Hindus, at least, are pretty confident that they can deceive the Reckoner of their deserts is illustrated by the familiar saying current in North India, that a certain man once stole an anvil, and hoped to make good his crime, by offering a needle in return!

Sometimes one hears that in Christian

countries a man who has done much harm to people by selling them strong drink, will try to make amends when he is old and near to death and the judgement, by erecting a hospital or an orphanage.

In this country a man tries to neutralize the evil of his life by digging wells, or by feeding Brahmans or ants.

Here is an old merchant, who has won his money by being always hard and sometimes dishonest. He knows that there is much against him, so he determines to try to turn the balance in his favour. He gives orders to have a deep masonry well dug for the public good. Or he will pay men to give water to the thirsty passer-by.

These men must be Brahmans, so that all can receive water from them without having their castes defiled. They are supplied with large earthenware pitchers which are filled with water, and with a brass cup for dipping it out. But this brass 'lota,' as it is called, is never put to a man's mouth. The drinker sits on his heels, curving his hands to make a cup, with the wrist to his mouth, and the water is then poured into his hands.

Considerable merit can also be obtained by feasting Brahmans, so the Brahmans say.

At these feasts the guests are fed with cakes, vegetables, and sweetmeats. Sugar, milk and curds are also supplied. The priests all sit on the ground, as they are not provided with, and do not require, chairs or tables. They have clean fingers, so they do not need spoons or knives or forks. They bring their own brass mugs, and their plates are made of leaves, fastened together by bits of dry straw. These plates are not expensive ; you can buy fourteen for a farthing, when they are in season.

After the priests have washed their hands, feet, and faces, the plates are distributed, and then the food is taken round. They eat in silence, reserving all their energies for their gastronomical exercise.

The size of the party depends upon the wealth of the host and the keenness of his

desire for merit. Any number of priests may be invited, so long as three or thirteen are not asked to the feast. These numbers are reckoned unlucky, as only at funeral ceremonies would they be welcome.

Some Hindus prefer to feed ants. It is not so costly as feeding priests. It is quite a common sight to see a tradesman in the early morning or evening, walking slowly along by the road-side on the look-out for ants. As soon as any are discovered, a little sugar or flour is put in their path, and then the seeker of merit passes on till the next colony or caravan is encountered.

It is also considered meritorious to release captive birds, which are captured for the purpose; to build temples; and to present cows to Brahmans. So the Brahmans teach. Feed and fee the Brahmans, eat the right food, marry the right woman, and you are a good Hindu.

As you have been told, the Hindu believes that by heaping up merit he will obtain salvation; and by that he means that he hopes he will be able to cut short the number of his transmigrations, which in the ordinary course of events, would number eight million four hundred thousand! The Hindu believes that he has lived before, and that at death his soul will migrate into some other body, it will put on other clothes. The sort of body it will get, the sort of robe it will wear, depends upon the sort of life he now lives; in the same way as his present state is the result of the way he has lived in the past. He believes that 'the soul may crawl as a snake, bloom as a flower, roam as a tiger, writhe like a demon, or reign as a god.'

In one of the sacred books of the Hindus, called *The Ordinances of Manu,* it is written, 'Those who eat what ought not to be eaten, become worms; . . . by stealing grain one becomes a mouse; . . . by stealing meat, a vulture; . . . by stealing fine perfumes, one becomes a musk-rat.

By bathing in the Ganges, by feeding Brahmans, by building temples, and in many other ways, the Hindu hopes his

soul will quickly escape from all bodies and robes, and become one with its divine source, as the river becomes one with the ocean.

One result of the belief in transmigration is, that, speaking generally, the afflicted and bereaved find no comforter. The leper and the widow are reaping as they have sown in some past life. They have got what they deserve; why, then, should they be pitied? Such is the logical outcome of this creed; but one likes to think that in the time of trouble many a widow and orphan has found that even the social tyranny of Hinduism cannot quench all a man's humanity.

The Hindu believes that the end of all, the best of all, the perfect life, is a dreamless, eternal sleep. And so he also believes that the perfect man is he who is most vacant and sleepy!

The Hindu saint wants less life and the Christian saint more. The Hindu saint seeks only his own release, the Christian saint would open all prison-doors. The Hindu saint is an egoist, the Christian saint a philanthropist. No one can live in Benares without seeing what blessings our religion would bring to these lives and praying that the Church at home may be roused to win India for Jesus Christ.

Published by

Facsimile Publisher
Ashok Vihar, Delhi-110052 (India)
Website: www.facsimilepublishers.com

Distributed by

Gyan Books Pvt. Ltd.
5, Ansari Road, Daryaganj, New Delhi-110002 (India)
E-mail: books@gyanbooks.com, Website: www.gyanbooks.com

9 789333 301527